THE DEVIL WEARS SCRUBS

FREIDA MCFADDEN

The Devil Wears Scrubs

ISBN-13: 978-1492177166

ISBN-10: 1492177164

They say every physician has a graveyard.

Mine may eventually contain Dr. Alyssa Morgan.

Watch out, Alyssa.

PROLOGUE
SOMETIME IN JULY

Time: 3 a.m.

Hours awake: 21

Chance of quitting: 75%

GEORGE LEEMAN IS MORBIDLY OBESE.

Before we got him in the bed, the nurses weighed Mr. Leeman on our bariatric scale. It's a scale we use for people who are either really obese or are in a wheelchair. The scale has a platform that's about the size of an elevator and you can wheel or waddle onto it. We got a weight for Mr. Leeman and used it to calculate his body mass index (BMI). The BMI is a calculation based on a patient's weight and height, and tells us scientifically exactly how overweight a patient is.

For example, before I started medical school, my BMI was 24. That put me square in the middle range of "normal." Now, less than one month into my intern year, my BMI is 26, which puts me just on the edge of "overweight," kind of like the rest of the country. If I continue to eat primarily junk food, which is likely given how the last few weeks are going, I might get up to 30, which would make me officially "obese."

Mr. Leeman's BMI is about five trillion.

Not really. But it's high—the highest I've ever seen. He's comfortably above the cutoff for morbidly obese.

What this means in practice is that he's got fat folds on his belly that are so deep, I could stick my whole fist inside. Hell, I think I could stick my whole *arm* inside. I think I might be able to set up a tent in his belly button with an adjacent fireplace. The nurses had to get him an extra-large bed because the regular hospital beds were too small to fit his massive frame.

I've been sitting here talking to Mr. Leeman for about thirty minutes, scribbling notes on a piece of paper about his heart disease, his medications, his other medical problems. I actually sort of like the guy. He's got a big toothy smile and he calls me "honey." I should probably be insulted by the "honey" thing since he's supposed to call me "doctor" and he's just being disrespectful and sexist, but at this hour of the morning, any kind words make me feel a little less awful.

My senior resident Alyssa particularly dislikes

obese patients. When the emergency room calls her about an obese patient, she sighs extra loudly. I'm not as bothered, and it's not just because I automatically like anything that makes Alyssa unhappy. But I figure nobody gets to 600 pounds just by eating a bunch of bacon double cheeseburgers. People who are that big must have a disease, just like the patients with pancreatic cancer or multiple sclerosis. And I'm not going to throw stones. After all, I like my bacon double cheeseburgers too.

"Do you have any more questions, sweetheart?" Mr. Leeman asks me. I've now graduated to sweetheart. He's making me feel all of twelve years old.

I look down at my page of chicken scratch. I can make out exactly five words on the page. I've been a doctor less than a month and I already got the handwriting down pat.

"No, I think that'll be all," I say. Then I add, "For now."

As a lowly medical intern, I must discuss every patient I see with my senior resident—and odds are twenty to one that Alyssa will send me back in here to ask something else I forgot. No matter how thorough a history I think I got, she always comes up with something. What's the patient's shoe size? What did he eat for dinner last night? What was the middle name of his best friend in third grade? Alyssa demands a very thorough history.

I find Alyssa sitting in the resident lounge, which is

her working area of choice when we're on call. She's wearing blue scrubs that make her eyes look bluer. Alyssa isn't beautiful, although sometimes I wish she were because it would give me another reason to hate her. She's on the cusp of beautiful, but she's a little too skinny, a little too tall, her forehead a little too long. My mother always says that the forehead is what makes the face. I'm not sure I agree with that one, but Alyssa's forehead definitely isn't doing her any favors.

Alyssa must be as sleep deprived as I am, but she doesn't look it. Her straight brown hair is swept back into… I think it's a chignon, although I truthfully don't know what the hell a chignon is. Not one little hair is out of place. Her eyes aren't bloodshot and don't have little purple circles under them, like I know mine do without even looking in a mirror. And she smells good. Nothing in this hospital smells good, except somehow Alyssa does.

"Hi," I say timidly.

Alyssa is flipping through her index cards. She carries around a pack of index cards on which she catalogues information about all our patients, and possibly one about me too. My biggest fantasy is stealing her index cards and watching her flounder. Then I get disgusted with myself that stealing index cards has now become my biggest fantasy. In any case, she doesn't look up from her cards when she speaks to me.

"Are you ready?" she asks me.

She's not really asking me if I'm ready. She's

really saying to me, "You better be ready and not be wasting my time, girlie." I wring my fists together and in the process, I crumple my notes slightly. Even though it's three in the morning, I've got a little surge of adrenaline going.

"I'm ready," I say, with all the finality of someone pledging her marriage vows.

Alyssa gestures at the couch across from her. I'm not allowed to actually sit *next* to her while we talk. I'm lucky she lets me sit at all. I can imagine her forcing me to stand at the doorway, maybe on one foot.

Before I can open my mouth, Alyssa says, "What took you so long?"

"Huh?" I say. I have no clue what she's talking about.

Alyssa finally raises her eyes from her index cards. "What took you so long?" she says again, louder this time.

My hands are sweaty. I wipe them on the couch and leave behind two little sweat stains. I'd be embarrassed if I wasn't so tired and also this couch is very possibly the dirtiest couch in the history of the world. Probably 20 years' worth of cafeteria food stains this couch. If anything, my sweat made it cleaner.

"I don't know what you mean," I finally admit.

"Connie got her last patient after you did, yet she presented him to me ten minutes ago," Alyssa says. She puts down her index cards and folds her arms across her chest. "Why are you so slow, Jane?"

Connie, like me, is a lowly intern in her first year of post medical school training. I secretly suspect that Connie and Alyssa are twins separated at birth. They even have that secret twin language where they look at each other and I can tell they're exchanging sentiments of how incompetent I am. Connie has conveniently provided Alyssa with a model of how to correctly do all the things I'm doing wrong.

"What are you doing that's slowing you down so much?" Alyssa says. It's three in the morning, yet she won't let this go.

I wrack my brain to think of an answer I can give that will end her line of questioning. I can't think of anything. I honestly didn't think I was that slow. Mr. Leeman is a complicated patient, more complicated than Connie's guy with chest-pain-that-was-clearly-indigestion. But I know that isn't going to be an acceptable answer for Alyssa.

"You need to work on being faster," Alyssa finally says. She clucks her tongue. "Well, go ahead."

I clear my throat. Around midnight, my throat always starts feeling scratchy and dry. I suppose it's just my naïve body telling me I need sleep. "Mr. Leeman is a 56-year-old man with a history of heart failure and diabetes who has been having increased shortness of breath for the last week…"

Alyssa takes notes as I talk about how the emergency room discovered that Mr. Leeman was having an exacerbation of his heart failure and his lungs were basically floating around in a swimming pool.

He got a strong diuretic that turned the swimming pool into a small Jacuzzi, and he is now doing okay, but still needs some oxygen. We'll probably need a few more days to clear out the pool. Then we'll send him home.

I launch into my physical exam findings. He has a heart murmur and lungs that sounds… well, wet. There's a sound that fluid-filled lungs make that now makes me think of the ocean. The ocean. I wonder if I'll ever have time to go to the beach again. Maybe Ryan and I can take the subway out to Brooklyn and… no, best not to think about it.

"What about his bottom?" Alyssa interrupts me.

"Huh?" I say. This seems to be my response to 90% of her questions.

"How did his buttocks look?" she says. "Any skin breakdown?"

"Uh," I say. "I didn't really…" I lower my eyes so that all I can see is my hands. "I didn't look."

"You're presenting a patient to me and you didn't even look at his buttocks?" Alyssa's usual monotone raises in intensity a few decibels. I can't imagine her being any angrier if I had suffocated the patient with his own pillow.

"I guess…" I bite my lip. "The thing is, he's really obese."

"All the more reason to look at his buttocks!"

"Yeah, but he can't roll over," I explain.

Alyssa gives this really loud sigh. Even Mr. Leeman one flight up can probably hear her sigh.

"Well, I don't know, Jane. How would you look at the backside of a patient who can't roll over on his own?"

"Huh?" I say.

Alyssa sighs again. She puts her pen down on the couch next to her and sits up a notch straighter. The girl always looks like she has a rod up her spine. When she speaks again, it's very slow, like the way she'd talk to a small child, if a small child had the misfortune of somehow getting into a conversation with her. "How. Would. You. Look. At. His. Backside. If. He. Can't. Roll. Over."

It's like one of those riddles where you've got two boats and five people and each boat can only fit two people and they have to get across a river in three steps or less. I was always terrible at those. "Um, how?"

"You ask a nurse to help turn him," she says, shaking her head at me.

A nurse. Great. Because they don't already hate me enough without my forcing them to turn a 600-pound man with about a trillion tubes and wires coming out of him.

"Okay," I say.

Alyssa has gone back to sifting through her index cards and I get a bad feeling. "You mean *now*?" I ask.

"When do you think, Jane? Next week?"

I can't believe Alyssa isn't going to let me finish presenting my patient to her. I can't believe I'm going to have to figure out a way to turn 600 pounds of flesh and bones (and lung fluid). This bites. All I can think of is my bed back home. My cozy bed with my down comforter and fluffy pillow.

I heave myself off the couch, resigning myself to the fact that not only am I not going to see my bed at home, I likely won't even get to see the creaky cot in the call room tonight. "Okay," I say. "I'll be back."

Alyssa doesn't even lift her eyes to acknowledge me.

When I get back upstairs to the floor where Mr. Leeman is staying, I head over to the nurse's station to recruit help. I see Rachel, a youngish nurse who doesn't seem to actively dislike me. Unlike Alyssa, Rachel really is beautiful, all dark and exotic. She has long black hair that she probably should wear in a ponytail, but it would be a crime not to leave it lush and flowing around her face.

"Hi, um, Rachel…" I begin.

Rachel smiles radiantly at me. "What can I do for you, 'Doctor'?"

Yeah, all the nurses call me "doctor" and I always, *always* hear the scare quotes. I don't blame them. I've been a doctor less than a month and I think it's kind of ridiculous they have to call me that while I call them by their first names.

"I need to turn Mr. Leeman to look at his backside," I say. I lower my eyes. "I'm *so* sorry."

Rachel whips her head around as she turns to the rest of the nurses, and her long black hair nearly smacks me in the face.

"We need to turn Mr. Leeman!" she calls out.

"I'm going to need some help. Angie, Maxine, Anthony, Katie, Julio, Jenny…"

I swear to God, she called out about ten names before she was done. A few minutes later, a parade of us are marching into Mr. Leeman's room. I'm still not entirely sure if we have enough manpower.

"Hello, Mr. Leeman," I say as we come into the room.

"Hi, sweetheart," he says as Rachel snickers.

"We're going to turn you and look at your back," I explain to him.

"Knock yourself out, kid."

Kid. Even better than *sweetheart.*

We arranged five people on one side and five on the other. After some degree of heaving, we manage to turn Mr. Leeman approximately 90 degrees. "Is that okay, 'Doctor'?" one of the nurses asks me.

As I draw my face closer, I smell it. It's not fungus. I know the smell of fungus better than I know my own name right now, being one of the most recognizable smells in the hospital (more on that later). But this is something else. Something horrible.

And then a second later I see it: a wound just at the base of his spine and to the left that is angry red and dripping with pus. God knows how deep that thing is. It may go down to the muscle or even the bone.

At this moment, I'm really furious. I don't know who I'm angrier at: Mr. Leeman, for having no idea that he has a huge smelly wound on his butt, or

Alyssa, for being right. Or the hospital, for picking me to work here for my three years of residency training.

And a second after that, I'm just tired. I don't want to deal with butt wounds. I just want to go home.

Hours Awake: 23
Chance of quitting: 90%

1

A FEW WEEKS EARLIER

THERE IS A DEFINITE POSSIBILITY THAT MY ROOMMATE is trying to kill me.

Why do I have a potentially homicidal roommate? It's pretty simple:

Fact #1: I work at County Hospital, located in a prime real estate venue in Manhattan.

Fact #2: As an intern, I earn a salary that only barely covers the cost of my medical school loans.

For these reasons, County Hospital has been kind enough to subsidize affordable dormitory-style housing for us medical residents. And this housing comes supplied with a random stranger to occupy the small apartment space with me.

I'm certainly in no position to refuse the dorm housing. The only alternative for me within my budget would have been renting out a cardboard box by the entrance to the hospital. And it would have had to be a very plain, no-frills cardboard box—nothing too nice.

The apartment rented to me is a step up from a cardboard box. Probably. It's slightly larger than a box, although it seems entirely possible there might be a box somewhere that's bigger than the room I'm sleeping in. The apartment, optimistically called "a two-bedroom suite," contains two adjacent bedrooms, a tiny bathroom, and a kitchen so small that I have to suck in my gut to get inside. The refrigerator only opens about 45 degrees before it bashes into the sink.

When I first moved in a few days ago, I was informed by the housing office that I'd be sharing the suite with a randomly selected female.

"What's her name?" I asked them.

"That's *confidential*," I was told.

Yes, they really said that.

So in summary, I have no idea who I've been living with the last several days, other than the fact that she is of the female persuasion. I'd love to officially introduce myself, but I've only caught brief glimpses of her. I hear a door slam and rush out to introduce myself, and poof, she's gone.

So all I know for sure is that she's evasive. And not particularly eager for me to know who she is.

I figure if I camp out in front of the bathroom, I'll eventually find her, but I'm too busy stressing out about starting my medicine internship in another day. I know I've got to organize my room because once I start my 30-hour shifts, I'll be too exhausted to move.

Most of what I've got in my room is books. Like, a million of them. I'm not a hoarder, but it would be accurate to say I've saved pretty much every medical book I've ever bought. Even the ones in fields I didn't go into like OB/GYN or Surgery. Because they're *books*. How can you get rid of a book? That's like throwing away *knowledge*.

Nearly everything else in the room is just furnishings provided by the dorm—a creaky desk, a wooden chair with one short leg, a single bed (including plastic-wrapped mattress), and a large bookcase now stuffed to the brim.

Aside from my clothes, the only other thing that's mine is Jack. He's my skeleton. Because you definitely can't be a doctor without a three-foot-tall skeleton in your room. Also, right now, Jack is the closest thing I've got to a boyfriend. If it gets any more serious, I may have to introduce him to my mother.

In any case, I have all my books unloaded and I'm starting on my meager wardrobe when I hear the pounding on my bedroom door.

I leap to open the door and I see her. My roommate. She's about my height and bone-thin with jet-black hair pulled back into the tightest ponytail I've ever seen. I can almost hear her hair follicles screaming in pain.

Also, she's holding a fork.

"Hi," I say. I was trying for enthusiasm, but I have to confess, the fork threw me off. "I'm Jane."

This is when a mentally-balanced person might

have introduced herself to me. Instead, the girl says, "Did you use my fork?"

Oh crap.

Okay, yes, I absolutely did use her fork. Here's the deal: I brought ten thousand books, but I forgot utensils. Clearly, I've got my priorities well-organized.

I have every intention of buying some forks in the near future, but last night, I had two options: eat spaghetti with my hands or borrow a fork from the dish rack next to mine. I would have asked, but I couldn't find my unnamed roommate anywhere. So I took the fork. I swear, I washed it after I used it. And I put it right back where I found it. But apparently, I was supposed to put it back facing North or some weird thing like that. I have no idea.

"Did you use my fork?" she asks again with a slight accent I can't quite identify. She shakes the fork in my face this time and I take a step back.

"Yes," I confess. "I did and… I'm *so* sorry. I forgot to buy forks."

"Okay," she says. She takes a deep breath, clearly trying to control her rage. "It was just weird because I knew the fork was moved, and I was like, that's weird, who would have moved my fork?"

"Yep, that was me," I say. "Sorry. My bad."

She points to the white handle on the fork. "See this white handle? That means it's mine."

"Got it," I say. "Again, I'm really sorry."

She nods. "Just remember, the white handle means it's mine."

"Okay," I say. She turns on her heel and marches down the hall toward her room. "Nice meeting you," I call, but she's already slammed the door behind her.

Damn. I still don't know her name.

2

JULY 1

Hours Awake: 1
Chance of Quitting: 22%

I HAVE BEEN A MEDICINE INTERN AT COUNTY Hospital for ten minutes and I am already horribly, hopelessly lost.

I am supposed to meet up with my new senior resident Alyssa and my co-intern Connie at 7:30 a.m. in the resident lounge. It is now 7:25 a.m. and I have no idea where the resident lounge is. I swear, I knew where it was last week when we had our orientation. It was on the third floor, right next to the telemetry unit.

But now the room that used to be the resident lounge is boarded up. There are literally wooden boards blocking the entrance to the room. How is this happening? I feel like I must be in some Twilight Zone where I'm about to discover I was never actually a doctor and this is all just some TV show I am starring in. (At this point, I'd be thrilled to discover that.)

I pace the dimly lit hallway about ten times, looking for any room that seems lounge-like in appearance. The floors have recently been mopped and are slightly wet and slippery—at one point, I catch myself seconds before my feet slide out from under me.

I return to the former resident lounge and just stare at the door for a full minute. Finally, I kick one of the wooden boards with one of my Dansko clogs, which is the official comfortable shoe of medical residents. Then I kick it again. Mostly because this is really frustrating and it's better than crying.

"You look lost," a voice says from behind me.

I turn around. A guy wearing light blue scrubs and a surgical mask is standing a few feet away from me. He's not wearing an ID badge, but I could just *smell* surgical resident on him. He emanates it. Also, and I really hate to say this, he's incredibly handsome. At least the part of him that isn't covered by the surgical mask is cute—he has intense blue eyes and a mop of dark blond hair. He's got muscles that I can even see under his scrubs, which is kind of amazing since I could be eight months pregnant under my scrubs and nobody would know. (Not that I foresee doing anything in the near future that might land me pregnant.)

Maybe he's horribly ugly under that mask though. Maybe he's got huge buck teeth and flared nostrils. I hope so, because it just wouldn't be fair for someone that handsome to also be a surgeon.

"I'm a little lost," I admit.

He pulls off the surgical mask, and damn, there are definitely no buck teeth or flared nostrils. He's actually very cute. Don't tell Jack.

"Let me guess," he says. "You're a Medicine Intern."

"Why do you say that?" I retort, even though obviously he's right. But my badge is flipped over, so he's got no proof.

He grins at me. Perfect white teeth, of course. When does he find time to brush? "Well, you're wearing a white coat, so you must be an intern. And the white coat is actually clean. Plus you're lost. Also..." He reaches out and tugs at the stethoscope around my neck. "I know you're from Medicine because you're wearing your stethoscope around your neck. Like a dog collar. You guys all do that."

Great. Sexy Surgeon just compared me to a dog. "Well, how do *you* wear your stethoscope?"

He snickers. "Why on earth would I wear a stethoscope?"

Seriously, I've had enough of this guy. It's hard enough to find the missing resident lounge without being taunted by an arrogant surgeon. I'm out of here.

"Wait," he says. "What are you looking for?"

I want to keep walking but I swallow my pride and say: "The medicine resident lounge."

Sexy Surgeon nods. "Oh, yeah. That moved."

No kidding.

"It's one floor down," he says.

"Thanks," I say.

He winks at me. "Good luck, Medicine Intern."

I'm not entirely sure, but as I step into the stairwell, I think I hear him say, "You're going to need it!"

————

I DO NEED IT.

I enter the resident lounge at 7:31 a.m., after spending at least thirty seconds trying to correctly punch in the code for the door (3-1-2). I am one minute late, but I can see from Alyssa's face that I may as well have arrived at half past noon.

"You're late," Dr. Alyssa Morgan snaps at me before I even introduce myself.

It's the first words she's ever spoken to me in person. We had a phone conversation the day before, when she told me to show up at 7:30 a.m. and she'd introduce me to my patients and orient me to the service. There was an impatient air to her voice, like I knew I had to listen to her very carefully because she would not be repeating *anything*.

In person, Alyssa just *oozes* impatience for some reason. Maybe it's the way her left leg crossed over her right bounces up and down as if she can't wait even one more minute. Or maybe it's the way she keeps looking down at her watch then glaring up at me. I've known Alyssa for 30 seconds and I'm already terrified of her.

It doesn't help that my co-intern Connie Lim is clearly a little shining orb of perfection. Connie has that fresh look of someone who very recently had a facial—her skin nearly glows. Also, unlike me, she's not wearing scrubs. She's dressed in a skirt and black boots, and actually looks *stylish* in her white coat. Connie is what they call a *preliminary intern*, which means that, unlike me, she'll only be doing a year of internal medicine. After that, she's going to do a residency in dermatology, which is one of the most competitive residencies in the country.

For the moment, I'll withhold my opinion of interns who are planning to do dermatology. You know how they say if you can't say something positive, don't say it at all? Yeah.

I settle down on the couch next to Connie and it creaks threateningly under my weight, which makes me feel like I weigh about a million pounds. I blame the couch, which is clearly very, very old. In fact, every item in the room looks like it should have been replaced a decade ago. The shelves on the splintery bookcase are sagging under the weight of several dozen dusty reference books. There's a copy machine that has an "out of order" sign on it that also looks rather dusty. The room has a single computer, which is the kind of early model you see in movies from the eighties and think, "Wow, did computers really used to look like that?" Even the window is covered in smudges—I'd imagine it's due to medical residents pressing their faces against the glass and wishing they were outside.

"I'm sorry," I finally say. I'm getting super good at apologizing lately.

Alyssa sighs and looks at her watch again, like she's considering just calling it a day at this point because I'm just so, so late.

Seriously, I am *one* minute late. Get over it, Alyssa.

"Connie and I already reviewed all her patients," Alyssa tells me.

They have? I'm one minute late. How did they have time to do that?

"So why don't you tell me about yours, Jane? How were they doing this morning?" Alyssa crosses and uncrosses her legs while she and Connie stare at me, waiting.

"Um," I say. "I thought that you and I were… going to… see them… you know, together?"

Alyssa looks aghast. "Are you saying that you didn't pre-round on your patients this morning?"

I look down at my hands, which are glistening with sweat. I wipe them off on my scrub pants. "I guess I didn't, no."

"Are you serious?" Alyssa asks me.

"I guess I misunderstood," I mumble.

Alyssa and Connie exchange looks. Neither of them can believe how dumb I am. I can just see

Connie itching to grab her phone to Tweet to all her friends: "My co-intern just screwed up big time!"

"If you didn't even see your patients," Alyssa says, "then how come you're so *late?*"

"I got lost—" I start to say, but then I can see that Alyssa doesn't really care about the answer to that question. It's clear that there's no excuse for not doing what Dr. Alyssa Morgan wants you to do. Even if what she wants you to do is apparently completely different from the thing that she said she wanted you to do.

———

MY FIRST PATIENT is a 63-year-old woman named Mary Coughlin. Mrs. Coughlin was admitted to the hospital with a kidney infection, but in the course of her work-up, we have discovered a mass in her pancreas. The mass could be *benign*—meaning, completely harmless. Or it could be pancreatic cancer, which is Really Bad.

Mrs. Coughlin is supposed to be very nice. So it's probably cancer.

The best part is that Mrs. Coughlin doesn't know about any of this yet. And even though I'm just meeting her for the first time today, I get to be the one to break the news to her.

Actually, the really best part is that Alyssa and

Connie are going to watch me do it.

Mrs. Coughlin's room is on the fourth floor. It's one of the busiest floors in the hospital, and I have to duck to avoid getting smacked by nurses hurrying by. Most of the staff is congregated in the nursing station, which is the central area where the patient charts, phones, and computers are located. I race after Alyssa as she makes a beeline for the nursing station.

"Did the oncology service leave a note on when we should do the biopsy?" Alyssa asks me, looking down at a white flash card she whips out of her pocket.

"Um," I say. "I don't know. We can check the chart."

Alyssa stares, gobsmacked. "You mean you haven't even *looked at the chart* yet?"

Sheesh. What part of "I thought we were all going to round together" is Alyssa not understanding?

I flip through Mrs. Coughlin's chart as fast as humanly possible, but it turns out it's hard to read quickly when there's an angry resident glaring at you and checking her watch over and over. Why check so frequently? It's going to be the same time as it was ten seconds ago.

As I get to the last page of the chart, Connie says to me, "Jane, what's that on your white coat?"

I just dry cleaned my white coat two days ago, knowing I probably wouldn't get much of a chance to wash it once I got entrenched in my intern year. So it's got to be clean. I've got to have *that* right, at least.

Except I notice that there's a sunflower of some sort sitting on the table next to me. I've been inadvertently leaning against it, and now there's yellow pollen *all over* the arm of my white coat. It looks like the flower vomited on me. I let out a screech and try to wipe it off, but that just spreads it around.

I cannot believe this. My clean white coat is now *covered* in yellow pollen.

"Clean it off later," Alyssa says to me. "We need to see Mrs. Coughlin now."

Mrs. Coughlin shares a double-room with a patient who is not mine, but is apparently suffering from nausea, because as we walk in, we all hear her retching behind the curtains separating their beds. Fortunately, Mrs. Coughlin doesn't seem to be bothered. When we reach her bedside, she's knitting, which is just about the cutest thing ever. She peers at us through the upper rim of her spectacles and smiles. "What can I do for you?"

Alyssa gives me a look, so I step forward. "I'm Dr. McGill," I say. It's the very first time I've referred to myself as a doctor. It feels *so weird*. My tongue can't seem to wrap itself around the words. I almost expect everyone to start snickering at me behind their hands that I just pretended I was really a doctor.

"Good for you!" Mrs. Coughlin says. "Are you still in training then?"

"Yes," I admit.

"And how long do you have left?"

"Three years," I say. Minus one day.

"How wonderful," Mrs. Coughlin says. "That will give you plenty of time to find a husband!"

I look over at Alyssa, who does not seem amused. "Dr. McGill is taking over for Dr. Reynolds," she explains.

"And what happened to Dr. Reynolds?" Mrs. Coughlin wants to know.

"He finished his internship," Alyssa says. "Dr. McGill will be your doctor from now on."

Mrs. Coughlin's eyes fill up with tears. "Oh no! But I really liked Dr. Reynolds! I'm going to miss him…"

Great. I've been this woman's doctor for about five minutes and I've already made her cry.

Connie expertly whips out a box of tissues as Mrs. Coughlin sobs over the fact that I'm now her doctor. This is mildly insulting. I may as well tell her about the tumor though, since she's already crying. Plus Alyssa is making a gesture with her hand like she wants me to wrap things up in here.

"Mrs. Coughlin?" I say. "There's something we need to talk to you about."

"Jane, dear," she says to me, reading the name off my ID badge. She's already decided she isn't going to call me "Doctor." And honestly, that's just fine with me. "What's that on your sleeve?"

I look down at my sleeve, which is now bright orange. Stupid flower!

"It's pollen from a sunflower," I explain.

"Oh, goodness!" Mrs. Coughlin exclaims. "I'm

allergic to pollen, you know." And then she sneezes loudly. But what am I supposed to do? Strip?

I clear my throat. "Listen, Mrs. Coughlin, I need to tell you that we did a scan of your abdomen and it turns out there's a mass in your pancreas."

I expect a fresh wave of tears but Mrs. Coughlin doesn't even react. "Okay," she finally says. She seems way less upset by the possibility of cancer than she was over finding out I was her doctor.

"The mass isn't that big," I go on. "But obviously we need to learn more about it. And we may need to do another scan to see if there are any more masses."

"Okay," Mrs. Coughlin says.

Wow, she is taking this *really* well. If I ever have a scary mass in my pancreas, I want to be just like her.

"Mrs. Coughlin," Alyssa says. "Do you know what a 'mass' is?"

Mrs. Coughlin shakes her head no.

Crap.

"It's a tumor," Alyssa says.

Mrs. Coughlin's eyes grow wide like saucers, then fill up again with tears. "You mean I have *cancer*?"

I'm sure she's going to burst into tears, but she doesn't. Instead, she starts sneezing violently and won't stop till I leave the room with my pollen-soaked clothing.

Hours Awake: 8
  Chance of Quitting: 45%

3

IT IS NOW CREEPING PAST 1:30 P.M. THERE ARE TWO things I have not done since I arrived at the hospital this morning:

1. Eaten
2. Used the bathroom

Alyssa and I are seeing a new hospital admission and I'm beginning to lose hope that I will ever escape from her long enough to perform either of these bodily functions. Does becoming a doctor mean I've given up my right to pee? I'm scared it has.

Note to self: Drink less coffee tomorrow morning.

My stomach lets out this super-human growl while I'm bending over my new patient to examine his abdomen. Super embarrassing.

The patient raises his eyebrows at me. "Was that you?"

"Just a little hungry," I say with a strangled laugh.

Alyssa, who has been watching me like a hawk from the other side of the bed as she writes little notes on an index card, cocks her finger at me. I follow her out of the room, and I see her brow is already creased in disapproval. I can't imagine what I've done wrong. Aside from *everything*, that is.

"Never tell a patient that you're hungry," she says.

"Why not?" I can't help but ask.

Alyssa blinks at me, as if stunned I had the nerve to question her words of wisdom. "It's unprofessional. Even a medical student should know that."

I just stare at her, and finally, she sighs.

"The cafeteria is going to close in ten minutes," she says. "Go grab some lunch and page me when you're done."

She doesn't have to tell me twice. I race down to the second floor to the cafeteria, making a brief pit stop to relieve my bladder. (Which feels glorious, by the way.) Then I head down to the cafeteria to eat the fastest lunch in the history of the world.

Hospital cafeterias are divided into two categories: Awful and Not-That-Awful. I have a bad feeling ours falls into the former category. There's a hot food option, which looks like soggy deep fried fish, with sides of mushy cauliflower and grayish rice. A salad bar would have been nice, but the only other option seems to be a bunch of pre-wrapped sandwiches.

I strongly suspect that these sandwiches are older than my medical school diploma, but I'm too hungry to care. I grab a random sandwich without even looking to see what's in it (chicken, I think) and a bottle of soda. I get in line, cursing the old man ahead of me, who is one of those guys who has to have a big conversation with the cashier. Something about his granddaughter and/or his prostate.

When it's finally my turn, the middle-aged female cashier rings me up and announces, "Four dollars, eight cents."

Four bucks for a crummy chicken sandwich and some soda? Are you kidding me? Don't they realize how poor I am?

I dig around in my white coat pocket, which are already clogged with gauze and scraps of paper and about twenty pens. But no wallet.

Oh crap. I forgot my wallet in my locker. This is just great.

"Hang on a second," I say to the irritated-looking cashier as I start rifling through all my many pockets, trying to gather coins. I fish out a dollar from one white coat pocket, a quarter and three pennies from the other. I check my scrub pockets and find only lint and a red button.

Why do I have a red button? I don't think I own anything red that has buttons on it.

In any case, it's not nearly enough. I can't even afford this crummy chicken sandwich. I'm seriously going to cry.

"I'll pay for her food," a voice says from behind me.

At this moment, there are no sweeter words in the English language. I whirl around to thank my savior, until I see who it is. It's Sexy Surgeon, now sans surgical mask.

"Thank you," I mumble, as he hands over the bills.

He grins at me. "How many times have I saved you today, Medicine Intern? Five... six times?"

"I'll pay you back for the sandwich," I say quickly.

He shakes his head. "I wouldn't hear of it. My treat." He cocks his head at me. "How's it going so far?"

"Great," I lie.

"That bad?" he laughs. He opens up the package of beef jerky he'd purchased and sticks one in his mouth.

"Is that your lunch?" I ask, incredulous.

"Oh, I don't eat lunch," he says, as if I'd suggested something crazy. "Surgeons are the camels of the hospital. I'm fine with one meal per day."

He'd get along great with Alyssa. Maybe I should set them up.

"What happened to your arm?" he asks me. He's staring at the sleeve of my white coat, which I drenched in water just after peeing, in attempt to get rid of the flower stains. Apparently, *nothing* gets out flower.

"I had an accident," I mumble.

Sexy Surgeon raises his light brown eyebrows at

me, but there's no way I'm going to tell him that I had an unfortunate encounter with a flower.

"Well, I'll see you around, Medicine Intern," he says. "I'll probably be by sometime later to save you again."

He takes off jogging out of the cafeteria, still chewing on jerky. Whether he likes it or not, I am going to pay him back those four dollars. I'm determined. The last thing I want is to owe money to Sexy Surgeon, no matter how sexy he is. No matter how great he looks in his blue scrubs.

Jane, stop staring at Sexy Surgeon and eat your lunch. Right now, Jane!

I pick the table nearest to the exit, even though it's stained with some sort of sticky brown sauce. I'm preparing to gobble down my chicken sandwich in one bite, except when I open the sandwich, it turns out that it's not chicken—it's tofu!

I hate tofu—really hate it. There's nothing intrinsically bad about it, but I just feel like I've been fooled by it too many times. There's nothing worse than thinking you're eating a piece of chicken and mid-chew realizing that it's actually tofu.

I'm glumly staring down at my sandwich when a tiny dark-haired girl with green scrubs and a white coat that's even whiter than mine used to be plops down across from me at the table. She looks like she's eight years old and playing doctor, but I suspect she's an intern, just like me.

"Mind if I join you?" she asks, even though she's already unwrapping her own sandwich.

"Sure," I say.

"Jane, right?" she asks me. "I remember you from the intern orientation."

"Right," I say. I don't remember her at all, but lucky for me, her badge is pointing the right way. Kali Castellano. "And you're Kali."

"Totally," she says. She grins at me with a tiny row of teeth. They make her look a little like an elf. I surreptitiously check for pointy ears, but her ears are normal. "Lay low. I'm trying to escape the other intern on my team."

I glance up and see… my roommate! She's wearing a white coat, her black hair still in that ultra-tight ponytail. I guess she's an intern too. "That's my roommate!"

"Poor you," Kali says, chomping down on her sandwich. "Oh God, this sandwich is awful! What is this—tofu? I thought it was ham!"

"Hey," I say. "Do you know her name?"

"Who?"

"The other intern on your team."

Kali frowns. "Wait, I thought you said she was your roommate?"

"Yeah, but she won't talk to me."

Kali laughs so hard that little pieces of tofu escape from her mouth. "Too funny! Her name is Julia. And she's very evil. I would lock your bedroom door at night."

"It doesn't lock."

"Then sleep with a knife in your bed." Kali chews thoughtfully. "I can't figure out her accent. I know she's an IMG, but I don't know what country she's from. There's no country I dislike enough to associate it with her."

An IMG is an International Medical Graduate, meaning she went to med school in a different country. It's usually hard for IMGs to find spots in American residency programs. Luckily for Julia, nobody is chomping the bit for spots at County Hospital.

"Maybe she went to med school on another *planet*," I suggest.

"Yes!" Kali cries. "She's an *Intergalactic* Medical Grad."

I laugh with Kali and it's the first time I've laughed all day. It feels nice, actually. I have a feeling it might be the last.

"Hey," Kali says. "Do you want to see my babies?"

And then Kali whips out her phone and I spend the next five minutes gulping down my sandwich (everything but the tofu) and looking at photos of Kali's cat and dog.

———

I DON'T EVEN QUITE MANAGE to finish my sandwich before I get paged. I'm still surprised by the sound of my pager. Last night, I tried to set it to the least grating beeping noise, but they were all pretty horrible. And I know that even if I find a sound that isn't intrinsically horrible, after a month, I will come to hate it with every fiber of my being.

I hurry to the first phone I see and answer the page. "This is 'Doctor' McGill," I say. It still feels so weird to say that. Will I ever get used to it?

"Jane?" It's Alyssa. Crap. "Where *are* you?"

I look down at my watch. Only ten minutes have passed since she gave me permission to go to the cafeteria.

"I'm getting lunch," I say. "You said I could."

"Right, I told you to *get* lunch," she says. "I didn't tell you that you could *eat* it."

What? Am I being punked here? Is she serious?

"I meant that you should get lunch and stash it somewhere for later," she says. "We're really busy, Jane."

"Right," I say. "Sorry. I must have misunderstood."

"Get over to the telemetry unit right now," Alyssa says. "Dr. Westin is ready to round with us."

Dr. Westin is the attending physician in charge of our team. In teaching hospitals, the hierarchy is that the senior residents are responsible for interns, and the attending is the old guy in charge of the whole team. The attending is a little like God:

1. He knows all.
2. He is *never* wrong.
3. There's only one of him.
4. When he says to do something, it is done.
5. If you screw up, he will unleash his wrath.

Actually, I'm not sure how wrathful Dr. Westin is since I've yet to meet him. But judging by past attendings I've worked with, I'd have to guess he's at least a little wrathful.

I find Dr. Westin sitting on the telemetry unit, flanked by Connie and Alyssa, who are both standing. Alyssa has her arms crossed and she's looking at her watch. How did everyone know we were meeting here but me? Couldn't someone have warned me about this?

Dr. Westin is thin and slightly balding, but still relatively fit and attractive for a man in his mid-forties. He has a kind face, but I refuse to be lured into letting down my guard. Unlike the residents, he is without a white coat, although like us, he's wearing his stethoscope like a dog collar (thanks for the analogy, Sexy Surgeon).

In normal human society, a man might have offered to give up his seat for one of three young ladies. But not an attending. I mean, you can't expect *God* to stand up and give you his seat, can you? That would be crazy.

If there's ever a seat available, there exists a very clear hierarchy of who may sit. First, the attending gets to sit. Then if there's another seat, the senior resident can sit. Then if there's another seat, someone can put their purse there. Then if there's another seat, a homeless drug addict who wandered into the building can sit there. But after the attending, the resident, the purse, and the homeless guy are all settled, any available seats are all mine.

When Alyssa spots me, she waves me over, all the while giving me the frowning of a lifetime. I sense an enormous sigh looming on the horizon. Dr. Westin waves to me with a broad smile on his face.

"Hello, Jean!" he says to me. "It's nice to meet you."

Crap. He called me by the wrong name. I freeze up, unsure what to do. I don't want our first interaction to be my correcting him. But I'm pretty sure I can't let him keep calling me by the wrong name for the next month. So I guess I have no choice but to say something. Right?

Right??

"It's Jane, actually," I finally say.

"Oh!" Dr. Westin seems a bit flustered and Alyssa gives me an accusatory look. The attending is always right, I know. But seriously, no matter how tired I am, I'm pretty sure I know my own name.

Maybe not though. Maybe Jean's better.

I notice that Dr. Westin is staring at the arm of my white coat, which is drying into a light yellow color. Stupid flower. I clear my throat and turn to the side, so that he can't see what a mess I am.

"Why don't we discuss Mr. Garrison?" Alyssa suggests, referring to my one telemetry patient.

"Excellent idea!" Dr. Westin exclaims. I really have to applaud his enthusiasm. I wouldn't have sounded that happy if Alyssa suggested we go outside for an ice cream break.

Mr. Garrison is a sick man, and that's why he's being monitored on 24-hour telemetry, which is essentially a bunch of electrodes that record the rhythm of your heart. He had esophageal cancer, and the chemotherapy caused him to go into heart failure, and now he's having arrhythmias. It's Alyssa's assessment that he needs a pacemaker. "Jane is going to arrange that," Alyssa tells Dr. Westin when I'm done presenting the patient.

I am? How do I arrange that? Couldn't *Jean* do it instead?

"Fantastic!" Dr. Westin says to Alyssa. "I think this young man will do very well." (Mr. Garrison is not young. He is 72. I'm not sure if Dr. Westin is being generous or if he misheard the patient's age.) "Jane, what medications do we have him on?"

Mr. Garrison is on a jillion medications. I realize that a jillion isn't a real number, but I really think a new number needs to be created to express the sheer number of medications this man is taking. I copied over the list in my pristine handwriting this morning and it covers two pages, which I hand over to Dr. Westin.

"Oh, my," Dr. Westin says, running his finger down the list. He adds, "My, my, my."

Dr. Westin's "My" Scale is renowned hospital-wide:

One My: Patient is mildly ill, likely discharge in next day or two

Two My's: Moderate illness. Patient probably needs some sort of invasive testing.

Three My's: Severe illness. Possibly close to ICU level of care. Intubation is imminent.

Four My's: Call the coroner.

When he finishes looking over the list, he beams at me. "All right then, let's pay this young man a visit!"

"He's 72!" is at the tip of my tongue, but I can't say it. You only get to correct an attending once in a lifetime and I already blew my one time by telling him my name wasn't Jean.

Dr. Westin leads the way to the room. I lag behind a little bit, and I feel Alyssa grab my arm. "Hey," she hisses. "What did you think you were doing back there?"

I stare at her, wide-eyed. She seems livid about something, although I can't imagine what. She already yelled at me for eating lunch. Was it the Jean/Jane thing?

"You're supposed to *read* the medication list to the attending," she says. Her brown eyes are flashing. "You don't just hand him the list. What's *wrong* with you?"

I don't have a second to respond before she whips

her head around and follows Dr. Westin down the hall. Is she right? I have no idea. At the time, the idea of reading off a jillion medications seemed crazy. I don't think I did anything wrong. But clearly, Alyssa disagrees.

And to make matters worse, I'm about 99% sure Dr. Westin is on his way to the wrong room.

My first hint is when he passes Mr. Garrison's room without even slowing down. But he seems so certain of himself that I feel like he *must* be the correct one, even though I found the patient in another room only an hour earlier. But after all, he's the attending. And *the attending is always right*.

When Dr. Westin finally stops, it's in front of a room with the name Lopez on the door. Alyssa looks like she wants to say something, but Dr. Westin has already marched inside.

The man inside the room is dark-skinned with jet-black hair. He really is young, maybe in his twenties. He looks surprised to see us when we enter. "Hello!" Dr. Westin booms. "I'm Dr. Westin."

Now I may not be the attending and it may just be my first day, but I'm almost certain this man is not Mr. Garrison. This guy is Mr. Lopez, or possibly *Señor* Lopez, and he is not one of our team's patients. I can't figure out why Alyssa hasn't said anything. She's got her mouth open, but can't seem to get the words out.

Well, if she's not going to tell him, I'm sure not going to.

"I'm very concerned about your heart," Dr. Westin tells Mr. Lopez. "We think you're probably going to need a pacemaker. I'd like to call the cardiology service to have it placed. If you don't do that, it could be very serious. You could even die."

Oh no. Dr. Westin is telling this young man, who is probably totally healthy (well, not *totally* healthy, since he's in the hospital) that he might die. This is bad. Alyssa, say something!

"Are you willing to consider getting a pacemaker?" Dr. Westin asks the patient.

Mr. Lopez stares at our attending for what feels like an eternity. Then finally, he says, "*Qué?*"

That seems to snap Alyssa out of her trance. She gently taps Dr. Westin on the arm, and says, "I think they may have moved his room. This is Mr. Lopez."

The patient nods vigorously. "Lopez. *Sí.*"

"My, my," Dr. Westin says, sounding a little annoyed.

After a brief apology (*lo siento?*), we make our way back down the hallway to Mr. Garrison's actual room. As we walk, I fall into step with Dr. Westin. He's much taller than me with longer legs, so I have to nearly jog to keep up. "Dr. Westin?"

"Yes, Jean?"

I'm Jean again, apparently. Whatever, let it go. Not worth it. "I just wanted to apologize for not reading you the list of patient medications earlier," I say. "From now on, I'll read you the list instead of handing it to you."

"Don't be silly!" Dr. Westin says. "I love that you wrote out the whole list! You have great handwriting, Jean."

Vindication! And a compliment! I flash Alyssa a triumphant look. In the short time I've been in this hospital, I have actually managed to do something right. Well, maybe not *right*. But at least not *wrong*.

But my victory is short-lived. Just as Dr. Westin is walking into the (correct) patient's room, Alyssa grabs me by the arm again. Her long, wiry fingers dig into my skin, even under my white coat. I worry she may draw blood. "I don't care what Dr. Westin says," she hisses at me. Her tongue is just the slightest bit pointy. "You *always* read the medications to the attending. Even a medical student knows that. Even a *child* knows that."

My, my, my, my.

Hours awake: 8
Chance of quitting: 63%

4
———

I ARRIVE HOME AT NEARLY 7 P.M. THAT NIGHT. CONNIE, against all odds, left the hospital at 3. How did this happen? Let me just say one thing: it is apparently not easy to arrange for a patient to get a pacemaker. It involves sitting on the phone for over an hour and being transferred between lots of different people, all of whom seem baffled as to why I was told that they were the one who places pacemakers. Eventually, I gave up for the day since nobody was answering phones anymore. I'm hoping tonight the pacemaker fairies will pay Mr. Garrison a magical visit.

I'm way too tired to even contemplate putting together a dinner for myself. Even a sandwich is too complicated. So on the way home, I buy a burrito at a sketchy Mexican takeout place. I suspect that eating the burrito in my room will be the highlight of my day, as long as it doesn't make me ill.

When I get back to my apartment, my roommate

(Julia!) is in the bathroom. I see the light on under the door. I know that Julia hasn't been super friendly to me, but I feel like since we're both interns, it's worth it to try to bond with her. I mean, she had to have had a bad day too, right?

I stand waiting in front of the bathroom door for an embarrassingly long amount of time before Julia yanks it open. Her hair is still in that severe ponytail— I wonder if she sleeps in it. She's clutching a roll of toilet paper in her left hand. At first I think she's stealing my toilet paper, but then I notice that my roll is still in place. Apparently, Julia and I will not be sharing toilet paper this year.

"Hi!" I say cheerfully.

Julia looks me up and down. I'm still wearing my scrubs, and the sleeve of my white coat has faded to a dull yellow. She narrows her eyes.

"Did you take one of my eggs?" she asks me.

I stare at her. "What?"

"I thought I had ten eggs," she says. "But now there are only nine. Did you take one?"

"No," I say.

I really didn't. I'm innocent this time.

But Julia doesn't look like she believes me. "Are you sure?" she presses me.

"Maybe it hatched and ran away?" I suggest.

Guess what? Julia does not think I'm funny.

In fact, she thinks I'm so un-funny that she pushes past me, and goes to her room. There are no locks on the door, so I know she's not locking it, but I imagine she's wedging a chair under the doorknob to make absolutely sure I don't ransack her room for eggs and forks tonight.

Days living with my crazy roommate: Too many
Chance either Julia or I will kill each other during the night: 38%

5

CALL #1

I AM ON CALL TONIGHT.

Call is this horrible thing that happens to you when you're a doctor. It essentially means that if there's an issue with one of the patients, the nurses can "call" you. All night long, baby.

In my residency program, interns are on call q4. What does that mean? Well, in medicine, "q" means "every" (it's probably a Latin thing) and "4" means "4". Put it all together and this means that I'm on call every four nights. Every four nights, I get to spend the entire night at the hospital answering questions about patients and admitting sick people.

To be honest, I'm the teensiest bit excited about it. I mean, this is what being a doctor is all about. This is what I've been waiting for. And now *I'm* the one in charge. I get to make important decisions, cure sickness, maybe even save lives. This is what I was writing about on that med school admissions essay.

(Excerpt from Jane McGill's med school admissions essay: *Illness is a treacherous dragon, breathing fire on innocent patients, and as a physician, I want to be the shining knight who battles that dragon and saves my patients' lives.*)

(No, really. I wrote that. In my defense, I was only 21 at the time.)

I enter the hospital at 7:25 a.m., wearing a fresh set of green scrubs and a new white coat that is as yet unstained. Today I'm definitely going to be on the lookout for flowers, that's for sure. I'm wearing my comfy Dansko clogs, knowing that I will probably spend the next 24+ hours on my feet.

Overnight calls in our hospital last 30 hours. Alyssa has told me to come no earlier than 7:30 a.m., so that I can stay until 1:30 p.m. tomorrow. County Hospital is very strict about us sticking to the 30-hour rule, because the hospital could get slapped with a big fine if we stay in the hospital longer than 30 hours. Along the line, someone discovered that tired residents perform at roughly the same level of competency as drunk people, so now there's something called the Bell Commission, which ensures there aren't a bunch of drunk people caring for patients.

In case you're interested in the history of the Bell Commission, it all dates back to the olden days of medicine. Back then, residents would go for weeks at a time without sleeping, eating, or using the bathroom. Sometimes *months* at a time. Truly, it was a golden age.

Anyway, this was all well and good, but then one day a woman named Libby Zion died in a hospital due to the tired resident missing a diagnosis. (Personally, I think stupidity could account for that just as well as exhaustion.) Zion happened to be the daughter of a big cheese reporter and it came as a huge revelation to the world that you can't perform competently while awake 35 hours in a row. But apparently, you *can* perform competently while awake 30 hours in a row.

It's all very scientific.

The elevator seems to be conspiring against me to make me late for meeting Alyssa. I'm standing there for at least five minutes, hopping impatiently between my feet. I probably look like I have to pee. At some point, an elderly couple passes me, and the wife nudges her husband and says, "Look! It's a little girl with a stethoscope."

This is not the best start to the day.

In the elevator, I run into my lunch buddy from yesterday, Kali. The second she steps inside, I sneeze violently. I can't help but notice she's covered in cat hairs. They are stuck to the back of her white coat, almost like she's grown a layer of fur.

"Hi, Jane!" she says. "Are you on call tonight too?"

"Uh huh," I say. I squint at her, wondering how to phrase my next thought as delicately as possible. "Um, are you keeping your cat in your dorm room?"

"No," Kali says, all wide-eyed innocence. "Of course not. That would be illegal."

"Um," I say again. "You've got cat hair on you."

Kali looks down at her scrub top. I shake my head

and do a spinning motion, so she wrenches her neck around to see the back of her coat. "Oh!"

"I won't tell anyone," I promise.

Kali lets out a breath. "Thanks, Jane. Honestly, I can't make it through this year without little Valsalva."

"Doesn't your roommate mind though?" I ask.

"I've got a single," Kali says.

Seriously, some people have all the luck.

————

Naturally, Alyssa and Connie are already waiting in the resident lounge when I show up. And what they're doing makes me ill: they're comparing diamonds.

No wonder Alyssa and Connie act like they're BFFs. They're both engaged. They can bond by talking about the fabulous weddings they're planning. Chicken or fish. Color schemes. Flowers. DJ vs. live band. The conversation topics are probably endless.

"Hi," I say as I walk in.

Alyssa barely glances up at me. "The diamond belonged to his mother," she's saying. "But we changed the setting. And I wanted platinum, of course."

"Of course!" Connie agrees.

Of course.

They spend the next five minutes talking in diamond jargon while I sit on the couch across from them and twiddle my thumbs. I suspect we would have spent the next 30 hours talking about diamonds, except then Alyssa's pager goes off. Her pager alert is the happy birthday song. Way to spoil every birthday I'll ever have, Alyssa.

"It's the ER with a new admission," Alyssa reports. She looks at me. "You're up, Jane."

"Goody!" Did I say that out loud? Alyssa looks at me funny.

Alyssa whips out an index card and takes notes as she says "uh huh" over and over again into the phone. She hangs up a minute later, and she's already glaring at me.

"I said you were up next," she says.

I just stare at her blankly.

She points her pen in my direction. "Why weren't you writing down information about the patient?"

"Because..." I feel like this answer is too obvious, that there's a trick that I'm missing. "They were talking to *you* on the phone. I couldn't hear them. So I couldn't write it down. That's why."

"And there's no other way you could have gotten the information, huh?" Alyssa waves her index card in my face. "No other way you could think of?"

"Um," I say. Did she really expect me to read her handwriting upside-down from three feet away?

"In the future," Alyssa says, "I expect you to copy down the information as I'm writing it. That way, we don't waste time."

"Time that could be better spent discussing diamond ring settings?" I say. No, I don't really say that. But I think it so vehemently that I'm sure Alyssa must be able to somehow hear it.

My first admission of the day is a Russian gentleman named Mikhail Petrovich. He is having chest pain. At least, we think he is. Nobody has yet located an interpreter. But apparently, he's clutching his chest and looking short of breath. So either he's having chest pain or he's just incredibly surprised.

This is my very first time in the ER, but it's hard to miss since the first floor of the hospital is plastered with arrows directing me there. It's apparently a busy day for the ER, because there are patients camped out in the hallway in stretchers, although many of them look like they're "sleeping it off." The stench of alcohol (not the rubbing kind) and old socks assaults my nostrils, and I start breathing through my mouth.

This place is a total pit.

As I'm slinking down the hallway, a guy lying on a stretcher grabs my elbow. I look down and see his fingernails are embedded with dirt. So are the creases on his face, actually.

"Are you a nurse?" he asks me.

I shake my head. "No."

He is undeterred by my response. "Do you work here?"

"Yes," I admit after a brief hesitation.

"Can I have some Percocet?" He offers me a hopeful smile.

"Let me find your nurse," I mumble, despite the fact that I have absolutely no intention of doing so. I detach his hand from my arm and see he's left behind a big dirty handprint on my fresh white coat. As I try to brush off the dirt, a stretcher nearly runs me down.

The high level of activity in the ER does not bode well for us, since we get our admissions from the ER. Busy ER = busy residents on call. So I better get a move on. I dodge a second stretcher rushing past me and attempt to locate Room 6, where Mr. Petrovich has taken residence.

I find Room 1 all right. Then Room 2. Then Room 3, 4, 5... and then the next room is Room 7. Is this some kind of sick joke?

I lift my eyes, scanning the room for someone who doesn't look like they're rushing to save someone's life. A nurse pushes past me with a full bag of dark red blood. At least I hope it's blood. Anyway, best to let her do her job.

My eyes finally settle on a familiar face: Sexy Surgeon! He's talking to a young woman in scrubs. As I approach them, I notice the woman is cowering a bit, and I can tell why: Sexy Surgeon is screaming at her.

"You're completely wasting my time, you realize that?" he snaps at her, his blue eyes flashing. "This is *obviously* a non-surgical abdomen. If you'd bothered to get a CT before you called me, you'd have been able to figure that out on your own. I mean, is everyone who works down here completely incapable of practicing basic medicine?"

Holy crap. Sexy Surgeon is a complete asshole.

Well, I guess that isn't too huge a surprise.

I try to slink away, but it's too late. He's spotted me. I freeze, but apparently he's not a T-Rex whose vision is based on movement.

"Medicine Intern!" he cries out. He actually looks pleased. The woman in scrubs takes this opportunity to slip away from him. She owes me big time. "What are you doing here?"

"An admission," I mumble.

"Is this your first ER admission?" He grins at me. "That is really cute."

"Thanks." I roll my eyes. "Listen, you don't... know where Room 6 is, do you?"

"Ah," he says. "The elusive Room 6. Oh, yes."

I can see a glint in his blue eyes. He's enjoying toying with me like this. I wonder if he finds one medicine intern to pick on every year.

"You see that crash cart over there?" he says, pointing to the cart stocked with supplies in case of the inevitable ER Code Blue.

"Yes..."

As he extends his arm, I can see the muscles popping out. Sexy Surgeon's got himself some nice biceps. But I'm not going to think about that. "Make a left at the crash cart, then it's at the end of that hallway."

"Thank you," I say.

"My pleasure, Medicine Intern," he says.

He may be cute, but if he calls me that one more time, I swear I'll punch him in the face.

———

NEARLY HALF AN HOUR LATER, I am no closer to getting a history on Mr. Petrovich. Mr. Petrovich is a disheveled man in his sixties, with tufts of gray hair protruding from his skull and his chest. He keeps moaning and clutching his chest. Whenever I try to ask him a question, hoping he's magically become proficient in English, he always answers the same way: "*Nyet*!"

I hate County Hospital.

I'm on the verge of tears when a man comes in with a big ID badge that says "Russian Interpreter" and declares his name to be Boris.

"Thank God you're here," I say.

"You may begin, Miss," Boris says in heavily accented English.

I don't bother to correct him by telling him that I'm *Doctor* McGill. Instead, I say, "Can you ask him where he feels pain?"

There's an exchange of Russian between Boris and my patient. I thought I asked a pretty simple question, but I swear they go back and forth like five times. "*Nyet*!" I hear Mr. Petrovich say.

"What did he say?" I ask.

"He said it's on the left side of his chest."

Five minutes of discussion for that answer? "And does it radiate into his arm?"

Another long exchange in Russian follows. At this rate, it's going to take me five hours to get a history on this man.

Boris hesitates. "To be honest, it's a little hard to understand him. I think he's speaking an unusual dialect. Also, he's mumbling a lot."

Mr. Petrovich is probably difficult to understand because he's *edentulous*, which means he has little to no teeth—where his teeth used to be, there are only gaping red holes. In medicine, we've got all sorts of fancy words for things that aren't very pleasant to say in plain English:

Emesis: Puke
Epistaxis: Nosebleed
Stool: Poop
Dyschezia: Hurts to poop
Hematochezia: Blood in poop

Boris and Mr. Petrovich converse for another few minutes while I stand there on the brink of tears. "*Nyet!*" I hear Mr. Petrovich say.

"What did he say?" I ask.

Boris at least has the decency to look apologetic. "He says his chest hurts."

"Great."

Hours awake: 5
Chance of quitting: 52%

6

_____

AN HOUR LATER, I'VE ORDERED THE GOLDEN WORK-UP for Mr. Petrovich. He's being admitted to our service to rule out a heart attack, and if he's not actively infarcting his heart, he'll get a stress test in the morning. I have no idea how they're going to explain to him what to do on the treadmill, but that's their problem.

I page Alyssa to go over the patient with me. She says she's back in the resident lounge, and I have to wonder if she's been there the whole time with Connie, discussing wedding rings. It's probably bad form to ask.

On my way to the lounge, I get a page and my stomach sinks. As part of my overnight call, I'm cross-covering the whole hospital. That means that if there's any problem with any patient in the hospital, I'm the gal who's supposed to solve it. It's kind of cool. And by "cool," I obviously mean it's completely terrifying and I want to curl up in a corner and hide under a big pile of coats.

There's a phone in the resident lounge, so I figure I can call back from there. I see Alyssa inside, sitting on the couch, waiting for me. Her legs and arms are both crossed.

"I have to return a page," I explain.

She nods. I've already displeased her.

I dial the number on my pager. "Hello, this is 'Doctor' McGill," I say.

I really need to stop doing those scare quotes.

"Hello, 'Doctor.' This is Jill on 3-South. I'm calling about the patient in Room 321A, Mr. Benson."

"Oh," I say. I did get a sign-out on this patient, which I stuffed in my pocket. I pull out a bunch of papers from my pocket and start rifling through them. "What's the problem?"

"We just checked his blood sugar," Jill says. "And it's 59."

"Oh," I say.

"What would you like to do, 'Doctor'?" Jill asks me.

"Um…" I look up at Alyssa, who is actively glaring at me right now. "Could we give him some orange juice?"

"He's NPO for a biopsy," Jill explains.

NPO means nothing by mouth. It's probably

another Latin thing. Anyway, how do you give a guy sugar if he can't take anything by mouth? Maybe I could give him some in the IV. But the guy's diabetic so I don't want to give him too much and send him into a diabetic coma.

"Hang on," I say to Jill. I cover the receiver of the phone and look up at Alyssa. "Um, this patient has a blood sugar of 59 but he's NPO. What should I do?"

Alyssa sighs really loudly. "You can give him one amp of D50."

I report this back to Jill, who probably knew what to do all along, then we hang up. I try to smile at Alyssa, who isn't having any of it. She gets out an index card and prepares to take notes.

"What are you waiting for?" she asks me.

"Sorry," I say. I clear my throat. "Mr. Petrovich is a 67-year-old man who…"

My pager goes off again.

Alyssa looks so unbelievably angry. Seriously, this is not my fault! I'm getting paged. How can I help it? This is part of my freaking job. I pick up the phone, swearing to myself that I'm at least going to sound like a real doctor this time. No scare quotes.

"Hello, this is 'Doctor' McGill."

Damn it!

"Hello, 'Doctor.' This is Marielle on 4-North. Mrs. Richardson was started on an ADA diet but no calories were specified."

I stare at the phone. "A… what? ADA?"

"A diabetic diet, 'Doctor,'" Marielle clarifies.

"Oh." Crap. I look up at Alyssa. I can see a vein starting to pulse in her large forehead. I'm probably going to give her stroke tonight. And I won't even know what to do, because I'm apparently completely incompetent. I brace myself. "Alyssa, this patient was put on an ADA diet, but they need to know how many calories."

"Is the patient overweight?" Alyssa asks. She sees my hesitation and shakes her head. "Never mind. Just tell her 1800 calories."

I report back to Marielle and then hang up the phone. Holy crap, this is hard. How am I going to get through the night without having Alyssa chained to my hip? I can't answer *any* of these stupid questions. And nobody's actually even sick yet.

For a minute, the two of us just sit there, staring at my pager, certain it's going to go off again. When it doesn't, I take a deep breath, look down at my notes, and start my presentation once again: "Mr. Petrovich is a 67-year-old man with a history of diabetes and hypertension who presented with substernal chest pain—"

Before I can get any further, I feel the notes being tugged from my hand. I look up and see Alyssa's angry face.

"Stop reading," she instructs me.

"Huh?" I say.

"Stop reading your notes," she repeats. "You

should be able to present the patient to me in your own words, without mumbling and looking down at the paper."

"Sorry," I mumble, looking down at the paper. I start over: "Mr. Petrovich is a 67-year-old man—"

"Show some enthusiasm," she says, pulling the paper clear out of my grip. "Have some inflection in your voice. It's very hard to listen to you like this."

Apparently, Alyssa expects me to do a dramatic presentation of Mr. Petrovich's chest pain.

I try my best to present the patient with a reasonable degree of theatrical enthusiasm. By some miracle, I manage to get through the rest of the patient presentation without getting paged again. Alyssa grills me as we go, but at least I have a ready excuse: my patient doesn't speak English and even the translator couldn't understand him. Short of him performing an interpretative dance, there was no way to get a more thorough history.

"All right," Alyssa finally says. "Why don't you go see if any of his labs are back yet?"

I go over to the computer in the room and log in as Alyssa continues to glare at me. I'm sure she's thinking that Connie would never dare present a patient to her that spoke no language dialect known to the human race.

The computer is taking forever to log me in. This is truly the slowest, oldest computer in the history of the world. Before our modern-day computers, people used calculators, and before that they used slide rules, and before that they used the abacus, and before that, they probably used this computer right here. The screen is about the size of my hand, and it has frozen up at least half of the times I've tried to log in to it. Fortunately, this time it allows me to successfully gain access. It must feel sorry for me.

I'm copying down the patient's labs when another intern I know vaguely from orientation enters the room. I glance at his badge and see his name is Rohit. He has huge dark circles under his eyes.

"Hey, Jane," he says. "How's it going?"

"All right," I say cautiously, glancing over at Alyssa. "Were you on call last night?"

Rohit nods. "Yeah. Unfortunately."

"How was it?"

"I don't want to talk about it," he mumbles, collapsing onto the filthy sofa next to me. "So are you taking sign-out? Someone told me you were."

"Yeah, sure," I say. "Just give me one minute to finish copying down these labs before the computer logs me out and I'll be right with you."

"No problem," Rohit says as he shuts his eyes and probably falls instantly asleep.

"*No*," Alyssa says, so sharply she jars Rohit awake. "Jane, he is post-call. Drop everything you're doing and let him sign out to you immediately."

"It's really okay," Rohit tries to say, but Alyssa has already crossed her arms and says, "*Now*, Jane."

Now, it is.

I sit down next to Rohit and he fumbles around in the pockets of his white coat to pull out his sign-out sheets. This is a list of all his patients, their major diagnoses, and what needs to be done overnight. The pages are littered with yellow sticky notes, explaining things that need to be done: follow-up results of CT scan, check recommendations from the renal service, etc.

"I don't think I've ever seen so many sticky notes in all my life," I say to Rohit, who laughs.

Alyssa, who is listening in, widens her eyes. "You have sticky notes, don't you, Jane?"

I do? No, I don't.

"No…" I say.

"You need to get some," Alyssa informs me. "It's very helpful to attach them to the sign-out sheet to help the person on call remember what they need to do."

"Got it," I say. Apparently, I'm going to be making a little post-call trip to the drug store to get some sticky notes.

When Rohit finishes going over the sign-out with me, I stuff the notes in my pocket, which I can tell Alyssa doesn't like. What does she want me to do— frame them?

"You need to learn to be more organized," Alyssa informs me.

This is going to be a really long night.

———

．　．　．

THE PATIENTS TRICKLE in after that. I'm conflicted in that I want to avoid being near Alyssa at all costs, but also terrified of being too far away from her because I don't know how to answer any of the nurses' questions. Well, I know how to answer *some* of the nurses' questions. Like when they ask me, "'Doctor,' have you written the admission orders yet on your patient?" The answer to that is no. I have not.

One thing County Hospital is teaching me is that I led a very sheltered life. I had absolutely no idea that meth was such a popular drug. Apparently, meth is the new… well, I don't even know what was popular before meth. I am just that uncool. But trust me, meth is really popular. At least among people who seek medical care at County Hospital.

Here's another thing I never heard of in my sheltered life: skin popping. That means injecting drugs directly under your skin. Sounds fun, right? Apparently, it gets you a better high than ingesting or snorting the drugs, and I guess it's easier than trying to find a vein. The only problem is that it's a great way to get an abscess. (An abscess is a big ball of pus. That's the official definition.)

At about 10 p.m., I meet Mr. Swanson, a 56-year-old man who has engaged in skin popping and now has a high fever and a huge abscess dangerously close to his groin. He also has a heart murmur that scares me a little bit, considering there's probably all sorts of bacteria floating around his bloodstream.

When Alyssa comes in to see Mr. Swanson with me in the admitting unit, I can tell she's impressed by the size of the abscess. It's the size of a tennis ball and deep red in color, located inches away from the line of his briefs, and he practically jumps off the bed when Alyssa puts her gloved fingers on it.

"This is too deep under the skin," she says. "I think we're going to need Surgery to drain this thing."

Translation: *Jane, stop daydreaming and call Surgery right now!*

Alyssa pulls her stethoscope from around her neck. She listens to Mr. Swanson's heart for a moment then looks at me accusingly.

"He has a *huge* heart murmur," she says.

"Right," I say. "I mentioned that."

"You didn't tell me how loud it was."

"Yeah, it's pretty loud," I admit.

"You can practically hear it across the room." Alyssa sighs and shakes her head at me. "You better order an echocardiogram too. Make sure the heart valve isn't infected."

"Okay," I say.

Alyssa looks me up and down. "Did you get those sticky notes yet?"

I stare at her. Did she *see* me leave the hospital and take a trip to the stationery store to buy a pack of stickys? "No," I have to tell her.

She shakes her head at me. "Make sure you get some."

As Alyssa flounces off to answer a page of her own, I quickly make a checklist of what I need to do:

1. Contact Surgery to drain big ball of pus
2. Order echocardiogram
3. Get sticky notes

No problem.

I locate a phone where I call the operator, figuring reaching Surgery will be the more challenging task.

"Hi, this is 'Doctor' McGill," I tell the operator. "Can you tell me who's on call for surgical consults tonight?"

"That would be Dr. Reilly," the operator says. "Do you want me to page him for you?"

"No, just give me his pager number," I say. I suspect it may take several tries to reach this Dr. Reilly.

I place a page to Dr. Reilly, and meanwhile flag down a nurse. She doesn't look thrilled to be bothered by yet another clueless "doctor."

"Hi," I say, trying to sound as nice and respectful as possible. You gotta be nice to the nurses. Or else. "Do you know what form I'm supposed to fill out to get an echocardiogram?"

The nurse narrows her eyes at me then word-lessly goes to a file cabinet. Since she didn't actually say anything to me, I'm not entirely sure if she's looking for the form or if she's looking for something that *she* needs and has just decided to ignore me. I stand there like an idiot for a minute until she finally plucks out a white form and hands it over to me, then leaves without another word. Maybe she was mute?

I look down at the form. It's got tons of check-boxes but none of them say "echocardiogram."

Also, Dr. Reilly hasn't called me back yet.

I page Dr. Reilly one more time while I sit and examine the form. How could it be this hard to order a simple echo? I mean, this is a test that gets ordered all the freaking time. It should be on every form! It shouldn't be some crazy puzzle.

I'm still mulling over the form when by some miracle, the phone next to me rings. My page has been returned!

"Hi!" I say excitedly, forgetting myself for a moment. I clear my throat. "Uh, this is 'Doctor' McGill."

I hear an irritable female voice on the other line. "I'm returning a page for Dr. Reilly."

"Oh," I say. "Um, are you Dr. Reilly?"

"No," she says. Obviously Dr. Reilly is too impor-tant to return pages himself. Also, I think I am learning to *hear* people rolling their eyes. "Dr. Reilly is *in surgery* right now. He can't be contacted."

"Well, I have a consult I need him to see," I explain.

"Well, he's in surgery," she says.

My head is starting to throb. "Can I leave a message for him?"

"No," she says. "You have to wait until the surgery is finished."

"Well, when will that be?"

"I'm not sure."

"But…" I bite my lip. "Isn't there supposed to be some way to contact him? I mean, what if there were a life or death emergency with a patient?"

"You can page him again after the surgery," the woman says.

It's becoming fairly obvious that this is a hopeless situation. Maybe I'll try again in an hour. It's not like I'm going to bed any time soon.

I hang up the phone and look back at the form. It hasn't miraculously filled out itself while I was on the phone.

There's a woman on the computer near me who doesn't look horribly busy. I approach her and clear my throat loudly a few times until she looks up. "Hi," I say. "Can you tell me what box to check to order an echo?"

She looks down at the form then up at me. "Transthoracic or transesophageal?"

"Um," I say. "Transthoracic?" Or the other one.

"That's the wrong form," she says.

Of course.

She goes back to the file cabinet and rifles around until she comes up with a new form, this one pink. She hands it over to me and I breathe a sigh of relief.

At least I will have accomplished one thing for Mr. Swanson.

I look down at the form. There's still no box for echocardiogram.

I might cry.

Hours awake: 17
Chance of quitting: 78%

7

You won't believe it, but eventually I do figure out how to fill out the form to order the echocardiogram. I end up having to recruit Alyssa's help, which she gives me only after a colossal sigh. And then she asks me if I've gotten sticky notes yet. I have not.

I'm less successful in contacting the elusive Dr. Reilly. I page him again at 2 a.m. from the resident lounge and get told by another irritable-sounding woman that he's still in surgery.

"Can you please tell him that we have a consult he needs to see?" I say. "The guy's pretty sick."

The woman puts down the phone and I sit there, my eyes shut, while I wait for a response.

"Dr. Reilly says to page the surgical consult pager tomorrow," she finally says.

"But I'm calling the consult *tonight!*" I cry. "The guy has a huge abscess and he's septic!"

I press my ear against the phone and I can just

barely make out a male voice saying, "Well, that's *her* problem."

I hate Dr. Reilly so much.

The worst part is that I'm not even sure I care anymore about Mr. Swanson. Mostly I just want to secure the consult to keep Alyssa from yelling at me. I'm not a terrible person—I swear. I'm just really tired.

After I hang up the phone, I just stare at it for a minute, trying to summon the strength to move. I still have one more admission to do before I even contemplate trying to get some sleep. I'm not sure I've ever been so tired in my whole life. I would pay a thousand dollars if I could go to sleep right now. Well, actually I wouldn't, since I don't have a thousand dollars. How about this—I'd give up a kidney if I could go to sleep right now.

Not that anyone is offering to trade.

My eyelids are slowly drifting downward when I hear the door bang open. I lift my head and see Kali stumble inside. She looks as tired as I feel.

"Jane," she says, managing a small smile. "You're not done, are you?"

"God no," I say.

"If you were, I'd have to hate you," she says. "I don't think I'm going to get to sleep at all tonight."

"Ditto."

"Julia might though," Kali says, crinkling her upturned nose. She collapses into a chair, cuddling against the armrest. "I would give anything if I could just not have to get out of this chair. I'd even give up, like, my spleen."

Pssh, just a *spleen*? Kidneys are way more important than spleens. She's clearly not as tired as I am. But I say, "I know what you mean."

She sighs and rubs her eyes. "I miss Valsalva. I hope she's okay all alone in my room."

"I'm sure she's fine," I say. Not that I'm basing that on anything. "Hey, Kali?"

She yawns. "Yeah?"

"Do you have any sticky notes?" I've got my fingers crossed.

Kali stares at me. "Any… what?"

"Sticky notes."

"Why on earth would I have sticky notes?"

Great question. "No reason. Never mind."

Apparently both Dr. Reilly and sticky notes are going to be out of my reach tonight.

————

At around 4:30 a.m., I'm finally wrapping things up for the night. I feel like 4 a.m. to 5 a.m. is that weird time that stands at the junction between when it's appropriate to go to sleep and when it's appropriate to wake up. But I've stopped caring about anything like that. If I have a chance to get any sleep tonight, I'm taking it. The adrenaline has officially run out.

"All right," Alyssa says to me, as she approves my orders on the final admission of the night. "We're going to meet up again with Dr. Westin to round at 7 a.m. You need to pre-round before that, but you can go to the call room and try to get a little sleep until then."

I love you, Alyssa. I want to give you a drunken hug.

I haven't yet seen the call rooms, but it says in my intern orientation booklet that they're located on the eighth floor. I'm sure I can manage to find them if I stumble around the eighth floor for long enough. I step into the elevator and prepare to press the button for the eighth floor and that's when I realize it:

There *is* no eighth floor.

I look at all the buttons. Floors one through seven are there. And that's it. Seven is the top floor. There's no eighth floor.

Apparently, I am going to be sleeping on the roof.

I'm still staring at the buttons when the elevator doors slide closed. I am so frustrated right now. I have only maybe two hours to sleep right now and I'm probably going to have to spend an hour of that time searching for the call room. If I find it at all.

Maybe I should just sleep on the couch in the resident lounge. Yes, it's disgusting. But at this point, I could just about sleep standing up. Maybe I'll just curl up right here in the elevator.

The doors to the elevator slide open and in walks Sexy Surgeon. It gives me some small degree of satisfaction to see he looks kind of tired too. His blue eyes are a little less bright and he's got dark circles under them. But he still manages a wide smile when he sees me.

"Medicine Intern!" he says. He's lucky I'm too tired to punch him. "How'd you survive your first call?"

"I don't want to talk about it," I mumble.

He laughs. "You can't be worse than *our* new interns."

I recall how Sexy Surgeon yelled at that woman in the ER. I guess there may be more painful things than having Alyssa as my senior resident.

"Hey," I say. "Do you know where the call rooms are?"

He nods. "Eighth floor."

I point to the elevator buttons. "And how exactly do I get to the eighth floor?"

"Oh, the elevator doesn't go there, of course," he says. Of course. "I mean, do you want patients' families randomly wandering into our call rooms?"

"I guess not," I grumble. "Well, how do you get there, then?"

"Elevator to seven, then go up the stairs," Sexy Surgeon says. He smiles at me. "I'm headed there myself. I'll show you the way."

I don't know if it's a show for my benefit, but Sexy Surgeon still seems to have a whole lot of energy for four in the morning. When we get to the stairs, he takes them two or three at a time up the two flights to the eighth floor. I'm taking them one at a time, clinging to the banister. I hear him yelling at the top, "Pick up the pace, Medicine Intern!"

Compared to the rest of hospital, the eighth floor is eerily quiet and dimly lit. There are no monitors beeping, no nurses rushing around, and no weird smells either. All I can hear is a low hum of the air conditioning. There are rows of doors, each labeled with a different designation. As I walk down the hall with Sexy Surgeon, he points out a room labeled "Senior Surgery Resident."

"That's me," he says.

"Oh," I say.

"Yours is probably down the hall somewhere," he says. He winks at me, "Of course, you're welcome to join me in here."

Oh my God, I can't believe he just said that to me. I have been awake for a billion hours and so has he and he's actually *hitting* on me? What an arrogant jerk. This is too insulting for words.

"Yeah, right," I say. "You don't even know my name."

"Sure I do," he says.

"Okay. What is it?"

I can see I've got him, but he still manages a cocky grin. "It's Medicine Intern."

Is this guy for real? "No, it's not."

"Um… Michelle?"

"No."

"Ingrid?"

"No!"

"Aphrodite?"

"Please stop guessing."

"Fine," he says. "What's your name?"

I hesitate. I don't want to get to know this guy, but then again, he's definitely helped me out a bunch of times tonight. And I don't want to be a bitch. Anyway, he'll figure it out soon enough.

"It's Jane," I say.

"Hi, Jane," he says. "I'm Ryan." He raises his eyebrows and cocks his head in the direction of his call room. "So… now that we know each other…"

"Go to hell, Ryan," I say.

He laughs. "Oh, well. Worth a try, right?"

Ryan disappears into his call room. As the door slams shut, I feel the tiniest twinge of… I don't know. Definitely not regret. The foremost thing on my mind right now is sleep.

Actually, it's too late now, but maybe Ryan could have helped me out with locating Dr. Reilly. I'd love to see Sexy Surgeon chew out the guy who's clearly been avoiding me all night. Maybe tomorrow.

I wander down the hall, passing the OB/GYN call rooms, until I get to a room labeled "Medicine Resident." My feet are barely holding me up at this point, so I open the door to the room.

The call room is very quiet and dark. It's warm—like a womb. There's no window, a single bed that's been recently made up, and a desk next to the bed with a phone on it. There's also a small attached bathroom. The room has pretty much everything I could need for the next two hours. It's perfect.

I set the alarm on my phone for 6:15 a.m., which is the latest I could possibly contemplate waking up the next morning. Then I kick off my shoes, and pull off my white coat and stethoscope and dump them on the desk. I slide under the covers of the bed. For a few moments, I worry that I'm going to get paged and woken up, but the lack of sleep quickly overcomes me, and I'm down for the count.

———

UNINTERRUPTED, I probably could have slept for the next two hours. Hell, make that 24 hours. But that isn't in the stars. Less than half an hour after I drift off, I'm awakened by the sound of the door to the call room creaking open and cold air flooding my cozy little womb.

For a second, I have no idea what's going on or where I am. Then it comes back to me: I'm an intern, I'm on call, and I'm in the call room. And the person at the door is Alyssa, for some reason.

"What are you *doing* in here?" she nearly screams at me.

I blink at her, and rub my eyes, squinting at the flood of light that's rushed in from the hallway. I don't get it. She *told* me to go to the call room to get some sleep. Did she mean she just wanted me to *store* the sleep for later, like for example, in three years from now?

"Huh?" I manage.

"Jane," she says. "What are you doing in *my* call room?"

"Oh," I mumble. "It said 'Medicine Resident' on the door, so…"

"Right," she says. "*I'm* the medicine resident. You're the intern. You take one of the *intern* rooms."

"Oh," I say. I add, "Sorry. I won't do it again."

"Get out of my call room," she says.

I blink at her. What? "What?" I say.

"This is *my* call room," she reiterates. "Go to *your* call room."

"What's the difference?"

"This one has a private bathroom."

Considering we have only about an hour left to sleep, I don't see how much it really matters, but I can tell Alyssa's not going to let this go. At this point, it's easier to just move. I shrug on my white coat, grab my stethoscope, and slide my feet back into my clogs. I trudge past Alyssa toward the door.

"Excuse me," Alyssa says. "You're just going to leave your dirty sheets on the bed?"

"I…" Baffled, I just shake my head. "What do you want me to do?"

"There are clean sheets in the hallway linen room," Alyssa says.

"Are you serious?" I ask.

Alyssa is dead serious.

So at five in the freaking morning, I go out in the hallway and grab a new sheet and blanket from the linen room, and I make Alyssa's bed. I even change her pillowcase, because I know she'll be horrified if I don't. The whole thing feels incredibly surreal.

"Fine," she says when I'm finished. My shoulders sag in relief. I was half-expecting her to make me retrieve a mint for the pillow. "You can go find a dirty linen bin to throw the old sheets."

I nod, even though I have no intention of doing so. When I find the call room that says "Medicine Intern," I'm going to throw the sheets on the floor. Someone else who's slept more than one hour can deal with this tomorrow.

"By the way," Alyssa says to me. "Did you get those sticky notes yet?"

Hours awake: 22 (give or take)
Chance of quitting: 83%

8

I STUMBLE OUT OF BED THE NEXT MORNING, MY ONE remaining hour of sleep having been interrupted by a call to inform me that a patient was allergic to Lithium. I hadn't ordered Lithium on this patient so I have no idea why this warranted an urgent 5 a.m. page, but I gave my verbal consent to add Lithium to the patient's allergy list. At least, I think I did. I only vaguely remember it, as if it were some kind of dream.

While in the communal bathroom, I brainstorm what I can do to make myself feel more like a human being. I readjust my ponytail, which helps very slightly. There's a travel-sized tube of toothpaste on the sink. I squeeze about half an inch of toothpaste onto my finger and start massaging my teeth. Funny how I feel more like I'm about to do the Walk of Shame after a sexy hook-up than finish my first shift as a doctor.

I quickly pre-round on my patients, which means I essentially look into their rooms to make sure they are still alive. Everyone is still alive. We've all somehow survived my first shift as an intern. Apparently, people are harder to kill than I thought.

I arrive at Dr. Westin's small office, where we're meeting to discuss our patients from the night before. Dr. Westin looks very chipper, especially compared to the three of us. He's clean-shaven, and his shirt is so blindingly white that I have to avert my tired eyes. He beams when he sees me, which almost makes up for the way Alyssa glares at me and looks at her watch.

"Did you have an exciting first night on call, Jess?" Dr. Westin asks me.

Apparently, I'm Jess now.

"Yes," I mumble as I sink into a chair in front of his desk. If there weren't a chair for me to sit in, I definitely would have cried. As is, I'm only barely keeping it together.

Connie, who apparently arrived an hour ago or something, has already reviewed her patients, so I'm up next. I tell Dr. Westin about Mr. Petrovich and his maybe chest pain, an elderly lady named Mrs. Thompson who has a mild kidney infection but seems better now, and Mr. Swanson and his abscess.

"What did Surgery say about the abscess?" Dr. Westin asks me.

I squirm. "I wasn't able to reach the consult resident last night."

Alyssa's eyes fly open. "Are you serious?"

"I paged him twice," I say lamely. And I realize that twice was not nearly enough. I should have been paging him every ten seconds all night long.

"I'll page him right now," I promise.

Alyssa just shakes her head. "You need to speak with him before you leave."

It's official. I will be spending the rest of my life in this hospital on this call.

After we pop in on my patients and Alyssa gives me a mile-long list of things to do, I slink away as quickly as I can. When I finish my to-do list, I can leave. Yet I don't know how I can possibly get through this nearly infinite list. I feel like Cinderella, when she was given that huge list of chores before the ball. I will never get to the ball at this rate.

The first thing I do is find a quiet spot on one of the wards and page Dr. Reilly again. After ten minutes, it's pretty clear he's not going to call me back. This asshole is wrecking my life right now.

And that's when I lose it.

I call Dr. Reilly's pager number again, but this time instead of leaving a callback number, I leave a voice message. "Dr. Reilly," I say. "This is Dr. McGill with Medicine. I have been calling you the entire night to talk to you about a patient who has an abscess and is extremely ill, and you have not had the courtesy to call me back. Apparently, you have absolutely no concern for patient welfare. I want you to know that I am going to report this behavior to your attending. If anything happens to this patient because you were unwilling to do your job, I intend for you to be found *personally* liable. Thank you very much." And then I hang up.

Holy crap. I didn't really say all that, did I?

Yet there was something cathartic about it. It felt good taking out my frustrations on another person. No wonder Sexy Surgeon enjoys it so much.

———

I'M DISCHARGING Mrs. Thompson with the kidney infection, which means I have to find the sheet to write out her discharge summary and medications. I go to 3-North, where Mrs. Thompson is located, and find a file cabinet in the back room that supposedly contains all the forms. I pull open the drawer to the file cabinet.

Wait. What was I looking for?

Oh right… discharge paperwork.

I start rifling through the papers: antibiotic forms, radiology forms, insulin sliding scales… oh my God, I am so tired…

Wait. What was I looking for?

Crap.

I check my notes. Right, discharge summary form.

I am really, really tired.

"Medicine Intern!"

I look up and see none other than Sexy Surgeon

himself standing in front of me. Or Ryan, I think he said his name was. His thick blond hair is slightly mussed and his scrubs a bit wrinkled, but other than that, there's no sign that he's been awake most of the night. I'm sure he hasn't spent the last ten minutes searching for a discharge form because he was too tired to think straight.

"Hey," I mumble.

"You look tired," he observes.

Gee, thanks. "Yeah, I'm kind of tired."

"Well, you're in luck," he says. "I've got a huge treat for you."

I raise my eyebrows. I admit, I'm intrigued.

Ryan grins at me, showing off his perfectly straight, white teeth. He's close enough that I can smell his minty breath. I wonder if he brought a toothbrush with him to the hospital. "In a few minutes," he says proudly, "you are going to get to see me *completely rip apart* one of your co-interns. I am going to *destroy* her. I'm going to make her *cry*, Jane. I'm going to make her wish she'd never been born."

And now I feel guilty because the idea of seeing someone else get yelled at is not entirely distasteful. I remember how good it felt when I let off some steam on Dr. Reilly. Maybe this is why everyone in medicine is so damn mean.

"So what horrible thing did this poor intern do?" I ask.

Ryan snorts. "You wouldn't even believe it. She left this really bitchy, completely inappropriate message on my pager. About how she was going to hold me *personally responsible* for her patient or some bullshit like that, just because I didn't return her page the second she snapped her fingers. I mean, she's a freaking *intern*. Can you believe the nerve?" He shakes his head. "You haven't seen Dr. McGill around, have you? Someone told me she was on this floor."

Oh no.

I am a complete idiot. Seriously. How in hell did I not realize that *Ryan* had to have been the surgery resident on call for consults last night? And now, for the first time, his badge is flipped around the right way and I can see his name. Ryan Reilly, MD.

I am so screwed. Sexy Surgeon is about to make me cry.

"I don't think I've seen her," I say carefully. I'm such an awful liar.

"Oh." Ryan frowns, disappointed. "Do you know where she went? The nurse on the phone said she was here like five minutes ago."

"Maybe the nurse was messing with you," I suggest.

Ryan laughs. "Oh, no. That would *never* happen."

Yeah, I'll just bet.

"Damn," he says. "Well, I'll catch up with her eventually. Too bad you won't get to see it."

"Too bad," I mumble. And the Academy Award goes to… Jane McGill!

And I almost get away with it. I am so close. Except at that moment, a tiny Filipina nurse named

Mary peeks her head into the back room and says to me, "Dr. McGill, you forgot to sign the order you wrote for Tylenol."

Ryan's eyes light up and he looks around for the elusive Dr. McGill. The whole thing would be almost amusing if it wasn't so terrifying. It actually takes him a good fifteen seconds before he realizes that we're the only two people in the room. That's when his face darkens. "*You…*"

"I am so sorry," I say. My voice has taken on an unattractively whiny, pleading tone. "I was paging you all night. And Alyssa was really mad at me that I couldn't reach you. I didn't realize that *you* were Dr. Reilly." I can't help but add for good measure: "And I'm *really* tired." I take a shaky breath. I wonder if I should get down on my knees and beg. "Please, *please* don't make me cry."

Ryan is just staring at me, still trying to decide how angry he should be with me. Finally, he shakes his head. "Okay."

"Okay?" I raise my eyebrows. "Meaning…?"

"Okay, I'll see your consult."

Well, gee, thanks for doing *your job*. Still, I am nothing but relieved. "Thanks."

"And I won't even yell at you," he adds, grinning now. He is way too handsome when he grins like that. And unfortunately, I'm pretty sure he knows it. Handsome surgeons are the worst. "On one condition…"

Oh great. "What is it?"

"I'm getting together with some other residents at

a bar tonight to get drinks," he says. "I want you to come with."

I stare at him. "Are you serious? We're post-call. I'm not going drinking."

Ryan snorts. "Come on, you're all of… what—26 years old? Nap for a few hours and you'll be good to go. We're not meeting till like eight o'clock."

"Well, forget it. I'm not going."

"Gee, that's too bad," he says. "I guess your patient is going to die of septic shock."

The really sad part is that I'm less worried about something bad happening to Mr. Swanson than I am about Alyssa yelling at me. "You're not serious."

Ryan folds his arms across his chest. "Try me."

He's not serious. He can't be.

Except he really might be. He's definitely a big enough asshole.

"Fine," I hiss at him. "I'll go get drinks with you tonight."

"I had a feeling you would," he comments, looking so self-satisfied that I wish I could smack him. He winks at me. "I hope this is a hell of an abscess, Dr. McGill."

I hope so too. But really, what do I know?

———

MY ONLY SMALL victory of the morning is that Ryan is impressed enough with the abscess that he agrees to take the patient to the OR to drain it. I'm really patting myself on the back for that one as I report the news to Alyssa as we "run the list" one last time in the resident lounge before I go home. "Running the list" seems to involve going through the checklist of all the things she told me to do so she can explain how I did each of those things wrong.

"Dr. Reilly is taking the patient to the OR this afternoon," I tell Alyssa.

Alyssa narrows her eyes at me. "And who's going to admit him back to the floor after he comes out of surgery? Do you expect *me* to do it?"

"No, Dr. Reilly said he'd keep the patient on the General Surgery service." And then Alyssa is left speechless. At this moment, I forgive Ryan Reilly for everything.

"All right," Alyssa says reluctantly. "Now let's see your discharge paperwork on Mrs. Thompson."

I hand over the stack of papers. I've handwritten a discharge summary, which includes a detailed account of how Mrs. Thompson had a fever and back pain, and we discovered it was due to a kidney infection, also known as *pyelonephritis*. I wrote about her exciting night on the ward of County Hospital. I left out the part where she yelled at me for waking her up "too goddamn early" this morning.

The next page is the list of medications we're sending her home with. I was careful to sign it, because I've now gotten paged at least a dozen times for forgetting to sign an order. You'd think I'd learn my lesson after the first eleven times, but no.

Alyssa looks over my paperwork. I already know I must have done something wrong, based on the way her narrow eyebrows are getting closer and closer together, but also based on the fact that I seem to be doing pretty much everything wrong lately.

Alyssa smacks down the list of medications in front of my face. "Did you forget something?"

"Um," I say. I look down at the list of Mrs. Thompson's medications. She's on a lot of medications, but I really thought I got them all. "No?"

She raises her eyebrows. "Are you sure?"

Based on the way she's saying it, it's pretty clear the answer is yes. But I feel like we may as well go one more round like this: "I don't think so."

Alyssa sighs. "You forgot to write for her antibiotic."

Wow. Okay, I have to admit, that was incredibly dumb. I mean, that was really, really stupid. A lady comes in for a kidney infection and I almost sent her home without antibiotics. In my defense, I'm pretty tired.

I quickly scribble an order for ciprofloxacin after taking way too long to double check the dosage as Alyssa continues to glare at me. "Sorry," I mumble.

She nods as if my stupidity comes as no surprise by this point. "And how about Mrs. Coughlin? Did you arrange for her biopsy?"

"Yes," I say. "Interventional radiology is coming by to do it this afternoon around three."

"Fine," Alyssa says as she makes a note about it on her index card. "By the way, you should go watch the biopsy."

My stomach sinks. In about 15 minutes, it will be 1:30 p.m., which means I'll have been in the hospital for 30 hours. After 30 hours, the rules state that I am allowed… nay, *required*, to go home.

Alyssa notices the look on my face and says, "I know it's painful to do these things post-call, but it's the best way to learn. You should try to go."

I may be afraid of Alyssa, but right now my exhaustion trumps my fear. The only way I'm going to that biopsy is if she hog-ties me, tosses me over her shoulder, and carries me there. Which isn't entirely out of the question.

"You can sign out first," Alyssa says.

"All right," I say.

"Did you get the sticky notes yet?"

I close my eyes for a brief second and an almost dizzying sensation comes over me. I wonder if I'll be allowed to leave this hospital without sticky notes. I fear not.

"No," I admit. "I didn't."

Alyssa looks incredibly disappointed.

"I can go to the drug store across the street and buy some?" I offer.

"Jane!" Her eyes widen in anger. "You are *not*

allowed to leave the hospital while on call. That is totally inappropriate!"

Then how the hell am I supposed to get sticky notes? "Sorry," I say. I feel like at this point, I should just write the word "SORRY" in big block letters on my scrubs. I can point to it and save my scratchy voice. Or I could write it on a sticky note, except I don't have any of those.

Alyssa sighs again. "I suppose you can go sign out now."

Believe me, she doesn't have to tell me twice. I race out of there like I've got ten minutes before I turn back into a pumpkin.

Hours awake: A jillion
Chance of quitting: 91%

9

I HAVE TO CONFESS: I SET MY PHONE ALARM TO GO OFF at 7 p.m., a full hour before I'm supposed to meet up with Ryan and his buddies. As much as I find Ryan completely obnoxious, there's also a part of me that finds him incredibly attractive and wouldn't mind at all if tonight ended in a few drunken smooches. My pride would take a hit, but it might still be worth it.

It's been a while since I've shared a drunken smooch, or any kind of smooch for that matter. When I was in my first year of med school, I was too over-whelmed to consider any kind of relationship. During second year, I started going out with a guy in my class named Joe. Everyone knew about me and Joe within two minutes of our first kiss, and when we broke up, it was Awkward (note the capital A)... so Awkward that I swore off dating anyone else in my class ever again. But where else was I supposed to meet guys? Med school was my whole life.

It didn't end up mattering so much though, since during third year, I was again too busy to even contemplate dating anyone. And in my final year, I was traveling the country like a nomad, never spending more than a month in any given city. The best time for a relationship always seemed to be "later."

Not that I want a relationship with Ryan Reilly. That's the last thing I want from the guy. And I'm pretty sure he feels the same way about me.

Still, I make an effort to look halfway decent. I shower, for starters. And brush my teeth with an honest-to-God toothbrush. I even blow dry my hair, so I look slightly less like a drowned cat. I rifle through my mostly unpacked luggage and pull out my make-up kit, discovering a thick layer of dust over my tubes of lipstick and mascara.

Here's a newsflash: Did you know make-up can *expire*?

I always thought it never expired. Like American cheese. But apparently, it really does if you keep it long enough. If you buy a bunch of make-up when you start medical school, but then your social life is so nonexistent that you still have that same make-up four years later, your mascara will be all gloopy and your eye shadow will have big clumps in it.

Oh well, I guess I'm going to have gloopy eyelashes tonight.

I figure anything I wear is going to be an improvement over the shapeless scrubs which are the only things that Ryan has yet seen me wearing. I'm banking on the fact that the July heat will support a tank top. I consider a skirt, but that reeks of trying too hard, so instead I opt for some cute boot cut blue jeans. And sandals with clunky three-inch heels. What can I say—I'm short.

The bar is a three-block walk from my apartment, which is just long enough to make me regret the heels a little bit. But when I enter the smoky bar, I'm grateful for my tank top. It's a sauna in here. The bar is one of those dark ones with sticky floors and tables, and big-boobed waitresses dressed in practically nothing. I can see why the surgery residents would like it here.

I see Ryan at a table in the back, flanked by two of his surgeon buddies. He's apparently had his eye on the door because he waves at me practically the second I walk in. I'm glad I didn't get too dressed up, considering all three of them are still wearing scrubs. I wonder how recently Ryan got off duty. Even though 30 hours is supposed to be the limit for calls, I know the surgery residents routinely break those rules. They take pride in it.

"Hello, Dr. McGill," Ryan says, grinning at me as I near the table. He lets out a low whistle when he catches sight of my outfit.

"Quit it, you," I say.

He laughs. "Guys, this is Jane. She's the young lady who left that lovely message on my pager this morning."

We exchange quick introductions but I quickly forget both the other guys' names because I'm awful with names. As I slide into an empty seat, the guy on my left, who has a mustache that makes him look a little like a sex offender, says to me, "That message? That was epic. Reilly's deserved that for like a year."

The other resident, who is very skinny with a huge Adam's apple and a bit of a Southern twang, says, "I think we're going to play the message at graduation."

"Oh, please don't," I say. "I was just… really tired."

"They're just joking," Ryan assures me. "They wouldn't really play it at graduation because they know I'd murder them."

Creepy Mustache laughs. "You don't scare us, Reilly."

A waitress comes by to take my drink order. The guys all order another beer and I get a Corona, promising myself that I'll stop with one. I'm already exhausted, and I'm afraid too much alcohol will either make me pass out or do something really regrettable. I reach into my purse to pay for the drink but Ryan shakes his head. "Don't worry about it, Jane."

I inhale sharply. "No, I don't want you to treat me."

"I'm not," he says, grinning at me. He jerks his head in the direction of his friends. "They lost a bet and now they have to pay for the next round."

I raise my eyebrows. "What was the bet?"

"They bet you wouldn't show up."

Suddenly, I feel a little dumb for having come out to a bar post-call. Nobody expected me to. Well, Ryan did. But that makes it even worse.

Creepy Mustache digs into his wallet and hands the waitress a clump of bills. He turns to me. "Ryan thinks he brought us here to be his wingmen, but really, we're here to try to talk you out of having anything to do with him."

"Do your worst," Ryan says. "I'm irresistible."

I roll my eyes.

"This guy," Southern Apple says to me, "is the biggest asshole in the whole hospital. Hands down. Trust me, we voted."

"Nice try," Ryan says. "But Jane already knows I'm the biggest asshole in the hospital." He folds his arms across his chest triumphantly. I can't help but notice the golden hairs on his muscular forearms and then I hate myself for thinking he's sexy even when he's acting all proud of being a jerk.

"Yeah, I know it," I admit. "I mean, that's why I left the message for him."

"Don't y'all worry, we're just getting warmed up," Southern Apple says.

Ryan leans back in his chair, not looking the slightest bit worried.

"I think it needs to be said," Creepy Mustache begins, "that Ryan has slept with just about everything female in the hospital. And I say every*thing* female. I'm including non-human animals in that."

"That's completely untrue," Ryan says to me. He winks. "At least, the animal part."

"Jane," Creepy Mustache says, "can you imagine what kind of sexually transmitted diseases this guy probably has? Gonorrhea, crabs… he probably even has the old-timey diseases like syphilis."

Ryan shrugs. "Hey, this is modern times. There are antibiotics."

"Not for herpes," Southern Apple points out.

"I don't have herpes, you idiot," Ryan says. He appeals to me, "I really don't."

Southern Apple looks me in the eyes and mouths the word "herpes" as Ryan slugs him in the arm.

"That's okay," I say, grinning in Ryan's direction. "I've already got a scorching case of it."

The other guys bust out laughing and Ryan just shakes his head. Apparently he isn't turned off by my alleged herpes. (I don't really have herpes, I promise.) In fact, as the guys continue to tick off reasons why I need to stay far away from Ryan Reilly, I feel his leg brush against mine. At first, I think it must be an accident, but then he doesn't move it away.

"Ryan's favorite movie is *Elf*," Creepy Mustache is saying. "You know, that movie where Will Ferrell plays an elf? That's his *favorite* movie. That's the kind of shit he's going to make you watch with him."

"It's true," Ryan admits. "But I don't think you seem like the kind of girl who's into chick flicks. Am I right, Jane?"

And when he says it, he nudges his foot against

mine. And goddamn it, my heart flutters in my chest. If I were hooked up to a telemetry machine now, they might need to admit me to the hospital.

"I like Will Ferrell," I admit.

Ryan grins. "What did I tell you?"

After we've been sitting there for over an hour, I feel like I'm going to nod off right at the table. I have to admit, I'm having fun, but I'm just too damn tired. It's almost like I spent the whole night awake.

"I'm going to head out," I say.

Creepy Mustache and Southern Apple both boo at me, but Ryan just says, "I'll walk you home."

"That's all right," I say. "It's only three blocks."

"It's a dangerous city," Ryan says.

I have this feeling that he's not going to take no for an answer, so I finally nod. "Okay. But just to my door. No funny stuff."

"Jane!" Ryan exclaims, mock offended. "What do you take me for?"

Hmm, maybe a guy who just boasted that he slept with every female in the hospital?

Ryan and I head out, his friends yelling after me, "Wear a condom!" Ryan turns back one last time to give them the finger then we're out the door.

Somehow the summer night air has cooled off considerably in the last hour and I'm feeling a little chilly in my tank top. I end up with goosebumps all over my arms, but I resist the urge to hug myself for warmth. I don't want Ryan to get any ideas, like that he should put his arm around me.

Or maybe I do.

"Hey," he says as he nudges my shoulder with his. His touch somehow makes the goosebumps multiply. "I got you something. A present."

I look at him in surprise. He reaches into the pocket of his scrubs and pulls out something square. Oh my God, it's sticky notes! Ryan's my hero!

"I heard you were looking for them," he says.

"Thank you!" I say, genuinely grateful for this gift of sticky notes. I tuck them safely into my pants pocket.

He winks at me. "Did I save you again?"

I hold my index finger and thumb a few millimeters apart. "Just a little."

He looks awfully proud of himself. "So you survived your first night of call, huh?" he says.

"Barely."

"It will get easier," he says, as he casually sidesteps the legs of a bum that are jutting out onto the sidewalk. "Then it will get harder again. Then you get your own minions to yell at, and that, let me tell you, is awesome."

I shake my head. "That's not going to be me. I'm going to be nice to my interns."

Ryan snorts at me. "Is that so, Dr. McGill? Like you were nice to the surgery consult resident?"

My cheeks grow warm, in spite of the cold night. "You don't know everything, you know."

I've stopped walking and so does he. We just stare at each other for a moment, while the goosebumps on my arm are breeding and building small colonies. Finally, Ryan says, "You look freezing."

"N-no, I'm not."

He takes me by the arm, his hand surprisingly warm against my bare skin. How could he be so warm when it's so damn cold out? "Come on," he says. "Only one block left. You can do it, Medicine Intern."

When we get to my dorm, he lets go of my arm to hold the door open for me. At this point I'm about 100% sure something is going to happen between us. I can tell by the way he held my arm, the way he looked at me as I walked through the door. It's pretty obvious that Ryan is used to getting what he wants, and for reasons I can't entirely explain, tonight he wants me. And, like he pointed out earlier, he's kind of irresistible.

We sprint up the stairs to my room, Ryan beating me by a few paces in order to allow him time to hold the door open for me once again. And then a few seconds later, we're outside the suite I share with Julia. We're staring at each other, with that post-date antici-pation, where you're waiting for the guy to make a move and you realize it's actually going to happen.

"So," Ryan says. His dark blond hair is tousled from the brisk walk outside, and God help me, I can see the tiniest bit of golden chest hair peeking out from under the vee of his scrub top that matches the color of the stubble on his chin.

"So," I reply.

"So that was fun wasn't it?" he says.

I wonder how far Ryan Reilly is going to get tonight. Now I sort of wish I hadn't shaved my legs, because I really won't have the will-power to stop him with perfectly smooth legs. Although in all honesty, that's kind of a myth. If you want a guy bad enough, neither of you give a crap about prickly legs.

"I had a little fun," I admit.

"Just a little?"

"Maybe a medium amount," I concede.

He nods. "That's better." Then he smiles. "Congratulations for making it through your first call of intern year."

And then he holds out his right hand to me. I shake it, wondering if this is some odd kind of foreplay. I'm embarrassed to admit my whole arm tingles a bit when we shake. I hate how into him I am.

"Well," he says with a sexy smile, "goodnight, Jane."

I expect him to lean in for a kiss at this point but he doesn't. He just stands there until I realize he's waiting for me to say something back.

"Um, goodnight," I say.

And then, you will never believe this:

He leaves!

Ryan Reilly, who has slept with every female in a ten mile radius, is about ten feet away from my bedroom and I am (let's face it) practically salivating over him, and what does he do? Nothing! He doesn't ravage me—he doesn't even try to kiss me. I don't get it.

Maybe my breath smells?

Maybe he decided my butt looks big?

Maybe between the bar and here he turned gay?

After Ryan disappears, I stand outside my suite for at least a full minute, wondering if maybe this is all a psych out and he's going to come back. Unlikely, yes, but not entirely impossible. But then it becomes obvious that he's gone for good, and I look like an idiot standing there. So I pop the lock open with my key, and open the door to the suite.

And I scream.

Julia is standing about two feet from the door. It is literally the creepiest thing I can imagine. Well, that's not true. It would be creepier if she were standing there and had dyed and cut her hair to look just like mine. But why would she do that? She hates me.

"You can't bring men into your room," she says accusingly.

I stare at her, then look to my left and right. I am quite definitely (and sadly) all alone. "Do you see any men?"

"You were with that surgery resident," Julia points out.

Okay, this is super creepy. "Were you *spying* on me?"

Julia doesn't say anything but just reiterates her point: "No men allowed in the room."

"That's not even true," I say.

Julia recites, as if memorized: "Tenants of the dormitories shall not invite unauthorized guests into the suites without explicit verbal or written approval of all other tenants occupying the suite."

"So I don't have your approval then?" I ask. I'm not sure why I'm provoking her. I must be meaner than I thought. Maybe Ryan is right about me.

"No, you do not," Julia says, answering as if it was a legitimate question.

Well, I don't think Julia's got much to worry about. Right now, I'm going to eat, sleep, and breathe internship. It doesn't look like there will be any "unauthorized guests" entering the suite any time soon.

10

CALL #2

TODAY WILL BE DIFFERENT. TODAY I WILL NOT MAKE any mistakes. I have my sticky notes. I will not give Alyssa any cause to yell at me. I will be the best intern who ever was.

Ha.

I have five patients going into my call and we're meeting Alyssa in the resident lounge at 8a.m. Even though I'm technically not supposed to arrive at the hospital until 7:30 for call to avoid breaking work hour rules, I come in at 7:15 because I am supposed to pre-round prior to our meeting, and I want to make sure I have all the information ready. I am just that dedicated.

I arrive at the lounge at 7:55 a.m., but Alyssa and Connie are both already there and acting like they've been waiting for hours. Alyssa looks at her watch and sighs loudly. I'm early, you know!

I plop down on the couch next to Connie. For

some reason, Connie only has one patient going into call, while I have five. How did this happen? I have no clue.

Connie is blessed, I think. She's the sort of person to whom good things always happen, and it's not clear whether she engineers it that way or she's just lucky. She has a very innocent look, with her layered black hair always pulled back in a thin pink headband and dimples I could stick my whole pinky inside. It's hard to imagine any treachery coming from Connie. Then again, she's a *dermatology resident*. (More on them later.)

Alyssa crosses her legs and glares at us. Well, she glares at me. She gives Connie a knowing smile.

"I was reviewing the history and physicals you wrote from the last call," Alyssa says. "And I wanted to give you both some feedback."

Alyssa whips out of her pocket photocopies of the notes that we'd written during our last call. I see my handwriting scribbled over with red pen, angry lines crossing through my sentences, often with only the commentary, "No!"

In the first paragraph, Alyssa has left only one word untouched. The word is "diabetes."

I look over at Connie's note. She received only a handful of red marks. A few times in the margin, Alyssa has written, "Good!" And once, "Great!"

This is not boding well for my call tonight.

"This needs a lot of work, Jane," Alyssa says to me, shaking her head in utter disappointment.

"Sorry," I say. I'm only five minutes into my call and I've already been forced to say that word.

"Did you pre-round on all your patients?" she asks me.

I nod. "Yep."

She squints at me. "When did you get here this morning?"

"At 7:15," I admit.

"You know," Alyssa says, "considering you're still learning your patients, you should be spending thirty minutes pre-rounding on every patient."

I do the math in my head. I have five patients and we were supposed to meet at 8 a.m.. So that means I'd have to arrive at the hospital at… 5:30 a.m.? But I'm not supposed to show up until 7:30 for call!

I turn this paradox over in my head, knowing that whatever answer Alyssa gives me probably isn't going to be satisfactory. Before I can say anything, Alyssa says, "Well, what's going on with your patients?"

Not a whole lot. Mrs. Coughlin's biopsy is still pending. Everyone is sick enough to be in the hospital, but not that sick. But I've got a handful of updates. "Mr. Chang's magnesium is low," I begin. "Should I give him some magnesium?"

Alyssa frowns. "Why *wouldn't* you give him magnesium? What would be the downside?"

"Nothing, I guess," I say.

She huffs at me. "Jane, you should know this by now. Replacing electrolytes is *your* responsibility, not mine."

"I understand," I say.

It would be great if she was going to let this go and let me continue talking about my patients, but I can see she isn't.

"Yesterday, I had to replete Mrs. Coughlin's calcium for you because you didn't do it," she says. "That is *not* my job."

"I understand."

"There's no harm in giving a patient a little extra calcium," she says. "Just, as you know, don't give it at the same time as phosphorus."

My eyes fly open. And… what do you do if you've already done that? Before I can figure out a way to delicately word that question, Alyssa's pager goes off.

It's the ER. We've got our first admission.

"You're up first, Jane," Alyssa says.

That means I need to keep track of what she's writing, so I don't waste a precious second of time. Except Alyssa has her index card at a weird angle and it's hard to read her handwriting upside down. Finally, I stand up to get a better look and I'm practically doubled over Alyssa, balanced on the toes of my clogs.

She cups the phone receiver and glares at me. "Jane, could you give me a little breathing room?"

"I can't see," I explain lamely.

Alyssa sighs and tilts her index card another five degrees toward me so I could read it.

My admission is Alexander Chandler, a 63-year-old man who is HIV positive and being admitted for shingles with severe pain. He's currently sitting in the ER, screaming in pain.

Joy.

At least this time I have no problem finding the room. I grab his ER chart outside the door, then gown and glove before I walk into my patient's room because he's on isolation precautions. The lights are out, and I see a man lying under a thin layer of sheets. He's taking slow, careful breaths and is covered in a thick sheen of perspiration.

He is also in fantastic condition for a 63 year old. I check the chart—he's 36. Apparently, I am not very good at reading upside-down.

Mr. Chandler's appearance is a surprise to me. Aside from being much younger than I thought, he's very clean-cut looking. His hair is clipped short, he doesn't have any tattoos or piercings, and he seems well-groomed despite his illness. I feel odd saying this but he's actually fairly attractive. Internally, I click off some of the reasons why he might have contracted HIV:

1. Sex
2. IV drugs
3. Transfusion
4. Needle stick

Mr. Chandler rolls his head in my direction and offers me the smallest hopeful smile. He says in a hoarse voice, "Are you my doctor?"

"Yes," I confirm. "I'm 'Doctor' McGill." Damn it, I still can't get rid of those scare quotes.

"Thank God," he says.

I have to say, this is the first time I've announced to a patient that I was their doctor and did not get met with some sign of disapproval or horror. I'm flattered.

"How are you feeling, Mr. Chandler?" I ask him.

"Alex," he corrects me.

I nod. "Sorry. Alex. Can you tell me how you're feeling?"

"Not so hot, Dr. McGill," he says, taking a shaky breath. "This hurts. A lot. I mean, a *lot*."

"Can I take a look?"

He nods his consent. I lift up his standard light blue hospital gown and I look for the lesions on the left side of his chest. Shingles, also known as herpes zoster, is a reactivation of the virus that causes chicken pox, and is not uncommon in patients who have impaired immune systems, such as people who are HIV-positive.

I see the red blisters clumped together in a wedge-shaped pattern over the front and back of his chest. They are arranged in a "dermatomal" distribution, meaning they follow the path of a spinal sensory nerve. I gently graze the blisters with my fingertips and he gasps in pain.

"Sorry," I say.

"It's okay," he says. I can almost hear him swallow

and there are tears in his eyes. "It's just… pretty tender. And the Tylenol isn't really cutting it."

I look down at Alex Chandler's chart and now it's my turn to gasp. He's right—all they've given him for pain is extra-strength Tylenol.

"That's completely unacceptable," I say.

He gives me a crooked smile. "Well, you know how it is. They figure I'm HIV-positive so I must be a drug addict."

"I'll get you some morphine," I promise him.

He nods. "Thank you, Dr. McGill. I really appreciate that."

I have to say, I find that kind of unacceptable. The guy has blisters all over his chest and is clearly in a lot of pain. I get that they're worried about drug seekers in the ER, but it seems to me that Alex Chandler has a right to something a little stronger than Tylenol. And I'm going to make sure he gets it.

Hours awake: 4
Chance of quitting: 12%

11

My second admission comes just before lunch. She's a 59-year-old black woman named Marquette Jefferson. She's actually a transfer from the surgery service, having presented with an infection of her left foot that spread to the bone. They took off her leg below the knee, but the infection persisted, so they did a revision of the amputation and now Mrs. Jefferson only has a quarter of her leg left.

It's not clear to me why we're getting her. She's sick, for sure—her diabetes is out of control, she's got heart failure, she's morbidly obese, and her kidney function is just short of dialysis. But it's not clear why she has to be in the hospital. But nobody can take care of her at home, and her insurance won't cover a nursing home, so somehow we're stuck with her.

Meaning *I'm* stuck with her.

Mrs. Jefferson is what's known as a "rock." A rock is a patient who will be on your service forever, who will never ever leave. Mrs. Jefferson is the rock to end all rocks.

She's a *rock star*.

But she's nice, at least. When I introduce myself to her, her wide face creases in a big smile. All my patients are happy to meet me today. It's a miracle. "Well, hello, darlin'," she says. Her hair is entirely gray, but her face is surprisingly unlined.

"Hello, Mrs. Jefferson," I say. "I'm Dr. McGill. How are you today?"

"Oh, just fine," she puffs, because her oxygen levels are not "just fine." They're more like "barely adequate."

I start the process of examining her. I place my stethoscope on her chest and hear the thump of a third heart sound—a sign of a failing heart. Her lungs sound mildly wet, but it's hard to hear much through all the layers of fat. Mrs. Jefferson smiles up at me and I see one of her top incisors is gold. "You have the prettiest red hair," she tells me.

"Thank you," I say. I almost cry at the realization that this may be the first compliment I've received since my intern year started.

"And a beautiful smile too," she says. "I bet the boys just love you."

"Not really." And I can't help but think of Sexy Surgeon. That one fizzled out quick. We haven't spoken since he snubbed me at my door. I have a feeling he won't be "saving" me tonight.

Then she adds, "You look just like my grand-daughter."

I pull off my stethoscope and stare at her. Mrs. Jefferson has charcoal-black skin, while I'm as pasty pale as a gallon of milk.

"Well," she amends. "She's black, of course. But other than that, you two could be twins."

Okay then.

After I'm done with Mrs. Jefferson, I discover that my first patient, Alex Chandler, has been moved up to a room on the main floor. I head over to see him, to make sure he's gotten a dose of acyclovir and is feeling more comfortable.

Chandler does look better than he did earlier. He's lying in bed, his brow still sweaty but not as markedly so. Again, I can't help but think to myself that he looks like someone I would have gone to school with. I suppose it's a mistake to stereotype people who get HIV. It can happen to anyone. Don't they always say that?

"You look better," I tell him.

He nods. "The morphine helped a lot. Thanks."

"No problem," I say. "It was criminal that they let you suffer like that."

"Yeah, well…" He sighs. "I'm HIV-positive, so obviously I'm a drug addict to them." He shifts in his bed and winces with pain. "You just don't realize how fast your life can turn around."

I've only got ten minutes before the cafeteria closes for lunch hours, but somehow this seems more important. Plus, I have to admit, I am super curious. How does a nice, clean-cut guy get HIV?

"What happened to you?" I ask.

"I'll tell you what happened to me," he says. "Never trust a woman." He laughs weakly then winces again. "Sorry. I'm bitter, I guess."

"It's okay," I assure him.

"My fiancé cheated on me," he says, shaking his head like he still can't believe it. "A bunch of times. Like an idiot, I didn't have a clue. Two months before the wedding, she tells me. She's HIV-positive. I never used a condom with her—I mean, why would I? She was almost my wife." He sighs, and rubs his face. "I was about to get married, I was an investment banker —I had everything going for me. That was three years ago, and now look at me."

I look at his face and see the dark circles under his eyes. I know he's on Medicaid. I wonder if he lost his job. I feel like it would be wrong to ask those questions, and all of a sudden, he groans and looks very uncomfortable again.

"Are you all right, Mr. Chandler?"

"No," he gasps. "This is… the worst pain ever. Christ."

"Do you need more morphine?" I ask. I calculate in my head how much he's gotten. I want to relieve his pain, but not stop him from breathing.

"Demerol has really helped me before," he says, between shallow breaths.

I nod then run out to write the order for Demerol.

More than ever, I feel determined to try to help this guy. After all, if this could happen to him, it could happen to anyone.

———

THE CAFETERIA IS CLOSED for lunch by the time I get down there. I almost cry until I remember the food cart parked in front of the hospital at all times. I know Alyssa has told me never to leave the hospital on penalty of death, but I think the food cart three yards away from the front door should be allowed. It's either that or faint from hunger.

As I get down to the lobby, I expect to smell the usual stomach-curdling aroma of fried food from the cart, but instead I smell nothing. There is a white cart parked in front of the hospital, but it's not the food cart. It's an ice cream truck—it's even playing the ice cream truck jingle. My choices right now include eating ice cream for lunch versus lasting another five to six hours without food.

I'm getting ice cream.

As I walk to the truck, I nearly slam into Kali, who is coming from the opposite direction. Meaning, she has done the unthinkable—she has left the hospital while on call.

"Oh!" Kali says when she sees it's me. Her cheeks turn pink. "Hi, Jane."

"Were you... outside?" I ask in a horrified whisper.

"No, of course not," Kali says. She tries to smile but keeps up the façade for exactly five seconds before breaking down. "Okay, I was. I went out. I *had* to."

I just stare at her.

"Val—you know, my cat?" Kali begins. I nod. "He's diabetic. He was all sluggish for a while and we couldn't figure it out. I thought it was his thyroid but it turned out—well, anyway. He's diabetic and needs daily insulin shots, so I have to sneak out when I'm on call to give it to him."

"You give your cat insulin shots?"

Kali nods. "Sure. It's no big deal. I just pull the skin away and he doesn't even feel it. It's actually very easy. For a while, we were doing fingersticks too to monitor his blood sugar, but I just can't anymore. I mean, I feel guilty about it, but as long as he gets the insulin, he should be okay."

I laugh. I can't help it—there's just something funny about imagining Kali giving her cat fingersticks. "Maybe you missed your calling as a veterinarian?"

"Oh no," Kali gasps. "I could never. It's way too sad when something bad happens to an animal." She frowns at the expression on my face. "That sounded bad, didn't it?"

"Slightly."

Her eyebrows scrunch together. "You won't tell on me, will you?"

"Of course not."

Kali sighs in relief. "Thanks, Jane. I'm not even worried about my senior resident. I'm just worried about that witch of a roommate of yours, Julia. She'd rat me out to the program director for sure." She looks over at the ice cream cart. "Let me buy you a popsicle."

I can't say no to that.

I take my sweet time selecting a popsicle, since this is apparently going to be my entire lunch. I haven't eaten a popsicle in a long time, probably years. They all look so delicious. Finally, I pick out the orange creamsicle. I'm practically salivating when they hand it to me.

Kali laughs. "Did you skip out on lunch today?"

"Am I that obvious?"

"The nurses usually will let you have some crackers from the nurse's station if they like you," Kali says.

"And what if they don't like you?"

We walk back into the hospital as I rip the wrapping off my popsicle and take a bite. It's so cold that it's a little bit agonizing to have it in my mouth, but I'm so hungry that it tastes like the best popsicle I've ever eaten in my whole life.

I hear a noise blaring over the loudspeakers: "Code Blue! 3-South, Room 318. Code Blue!"

Kali looks at me. "Aren't you part of the code team tonight?"

Shit, she's right.

And then I start running.

Hospitals are all about codes, and I spent several hours during orientation learning all of them:

Code Red: There's a fire! Run for your life! (Or save patients, whatever.)

Code Yellow: Bomb threat. Holy crap.

Code Dr. Strong: Someone is beating someone else up.

Most of the codes vary between different hospitals, but Code Blue is pretty universal. It means someone is maybe dying and needs to be resuscitated. And I'm supposed to save them. Somehow.

Prior to my intern year, I took a course called Advanced Cardiac Life Support. Basically, it teaches you how to run a Code Blue. It teaches you how to give a patient's heart an electric shock and administer life-saving medications. After the course, we took a test and I got 100%. I was so proud of myself.

That was about two weeks ago. I've now forgotten every single thing I learned in the class and I have absolutely no idea what I'm going to do at this code.

I run up the stairs because *there's just no time to wait for the elevator*. I mean, how embarrassing would it be if I'm twiddling my thumbs at the elevator while a patient is in ventricular fibrillation? But the consequence is that when I arrive at the third floor, I'm seriously out of breath. I have to hold onto the wall for a minute while I cough and gasp for air. This is kind of pathetic. I'm beginning to worry they might need to call a Code Blue on *me*.

I do manage to catch my breath though, and I

make my way to Room 318. The patient isn't one of ours—it's a man I've never seen before. He's extremely yellow. I don't think I've ever seen a non-cartoon human being quite so yellow in my life. He's almost glowing.

He's got IVs coming out of both arms, and pads on his chest to prepare for electric shocks if needed. Right now, there's a male nurse pumping on his chest, as another nurse manually gives him oxygen.

Dr. Westin is at the head of the bed, running the code. Alyssa is a few steps back, watching him run the code. I'm pleased to find that I beat out Connie, who is nowhere in sight.

"Hey," I whisper to Alyssa, eager to point out my promptness. "I'm here."

Alyssa turns. She gives me an utterly disgusted look. "Are you holding a *popsicle*?"

Yes. Yes, I am.

Between my hunger and my eagerness to get to the code, I guess I never ended up throwing away my orange creamsicle. So here I am, in the middle of this patient being resuscitated, clutching a popsicle in my left hand. I'd probably be better off if I never came at all.

"Sorry," I say.

A nurse taps me on the shoulder. I can tell she's angry by the aggressive way she taps me.

"Did you do that?" she asks, pointing at the floor.

Okay, so not only did I bring a popsicle to a code, but the popsicle has been dripping all the way here.

I've left a little trail of orange and vanilla ice cream behind me on the floor. It leads all the way off the unit.

"Yes," I admit, hanging my head.

"Clean it up," she orders me.

Connie arrives a minute later and gets to do chest compressions. Whereas I spend the rest of the code on my knees with paper towels, cleaning up the trail of ice cream.

Hours awake: 8
Chance of quitting: 47%

12

"TELL ME ABOUT YOUR LAST ADMISSION," ALYSSA SAYS to me.

The Code Blue is over. The patient was intubated and swept off to the ICU in critical but stable condition. He's not dead is all I know. Now we're sitting on 3-South, my popsicle is long gone, and I'm starving. But at least I'm not tired and I don't have to pee. I figure I'm always going to be ignoring at least one of my body's needs.

"Okay," I say. I fumble in my white coat pocket for my notes, but then I remember how Alyssa hates it when I *read* my notes, so I decide to wing it. "Mrs. Washington is a 59-year-old female who—"

"Who?"

I hesitate. Crap, wrong President. This wouldn't have happened if Alyssa would let me read my notes when I present to her. "I mean, Mrs. *Jefferson* is a 59-year-old female who—"

"Don't say 'female,'" Alyssa interrupts me.

"Huh?"

"When you call her a 'female,' what do you mean by that? What is she—a female dog? A female horse?"

I stare at Alyssa. "No, she's a female human."

"Right, and what's the word for that?"

I bite my lip. Is this a trick question?

Alyssa rolls her eyes. "A *woman*, right?"

"Oh. Right."

Alyssa sighs. "Go ahead."

"Um," I say. "Mrs. Jefferson is a 59-year-old *woman* who—"

Apparently, I'm not destined to say anything more than that first half-sentence because that's when Alyssa's pager goes off. She goes to answer it, eying me like I might scurry off if she's not careful. As if I'd have the courage to walk away from Alyssa.

I don't know what this phone call is about, but it's not from the ER and it's upsetting her even more than my calling Mrs. Jefferson a female.

"How much?" she barks into the phone. "No, you're right, that *is* a lot. Absolutely, I agree. No more than that. My intern will go talk to him."

Alyssa slams down the phone. "Jane," she says. "You are giving Mr. Chandler *way* too much narcotics. We're cutting him off right now."

"He's in pain though," I protest. "Don't we have to treat his pain?"

"I'm not going to sit here and argue with you, Jane," she says. "Go talk to him and tell him to stop bothering the nurses for pain meds. He can have what's already prescribed, nothing more."

"But what about Mrs. Jackson?" I ask.

"*Who?*"

Crap, wrong President. Again.

"I mean, Mrs. Jefferson," I correct myself.

"No, you need to go take care of Chandler right now," Alyssa says. "He's giving the nurses hell."

I can't even imagine such a thing. I'm beginning to get familiar with the nurses on that unit and they tend to be a bit lazy. I can imagine that they're sick of fetching pain meds for Mr. Chandler, so their solution is to call him a baby and rat him out to my superior. Still, I've got to do what Alyssa says.

When I reach Alex Chandler's room, he's got the lights out again and he's watching television. He shuts it off when I enter the room. He flashes me the tiniest of smiles as I gown up to go inside.

"Did I get you in trouble?" he asks.

"No," I lie. "But… I think we have to cut back on the pain meds. A little."

Alex nods. "That's okay. I… I think I can get through it."

This is the guy that was giving the nurses hell? Seriously?

"I'm just kind of itchy," he says, shrugging helplessly. "Like, all over. Do you think you Benadryl might help for that?"

"I can give you Benadryl," I say, thrilled to be able

to offer him something that isn't a controlled substance.

"Thanks," he says. And he just seems *so* grateful.

"No problem," I say.

I can't help but imagine what it would be like to have the dumb bad luck Alex Chandler had, end up with an incurable disease, then find myself in the hospital and in pain. I know I'd want my doctor to be nice to me.

———

I GET PAGED PRACTICALLY the second I sit down in the cafeteria for dinner with Kali and a few other interns. I look down at my tray of food. I haven't eaten since breakfast, so I bought food with that in mind. I've got fried chicken, rice, mashed potatoes, a garlic roll, and a big bottle of Diet Coke. On top of that, I bought two huge bags of chips. By the end of my intern year, I'm going to be as big as Mrs. Lincoln. I mean, Mrs. Jefferson.

I return the page from my cell phone, even though the reception is spotty. I just don't have the energy to get up. I hear Alyssa's voice on the other line, which is almost enough to make me lose my appetite. Almost.

"I've got your third admission for you," she says. "Come meet me in the resident lounge."

"Can't you just tell me about him over the phone?" I ask.

Alyssa doesn't say anything.

"Because I was about to eat dinner…" I begin. Then I realize this line of argument is pointless. Alyssa doesn't believe in eating. "Okay, I'll be right there."

"Who was that?" Kali asks me.

"Alyssa," I say. "She wants me to come to the resident lounge right now."

Kali's eyes widen. "No. Jane, you are going to eat your dinner. I am not going to allow you to leave this table before you eat at least one drumstick and five… no, *eight* bites of mashed potatoes. Eat your food, young lady."

I smile gratefully at Kali. She's right—Alyssa can wait. After all, she's going to be pissed off at me no matter what. I may as well eat.

I proceed to shove food into my throat so rapidly that I feel like I'm in one of those contests where they're trying to see who can eat fifty hot dogs faster, a man or a bear. (The bear always wins because it doesn't need to chew.) I swallow half my cola in one gulp, grab my two bags of chips, and hurry down to the resident lounge.

I'm already bracing myself to get chewed out by Alyssa, but when I get to the lounge, she's on the phone. She's got her cell phone pressed against her ear and she's actually smiling a little. I didn't even know her facial muscles were capable of doing that.

"I love you, sweetie," she coos into the phone. "I love you so much. I love you more than the moon and the stars and the planets and the whole universe."

Oh God. I definitely wouldn't have pegged Alyssa as the kind of girlfriend who got mushy on the phone. Next thing she's going to start calling her boyfriend pet names like "schmoopy." This is nauseating to listen to. Especially after the way Sexy Surgeon rejected me the other night. Nobody will ever call *me* schmoopy.

"Good night, sweetie," she says into the phone. "Mommy will see you tomorrow."

Mommy?

Alyssa's a mom? I didn't even realize she was married yet.

She makes kissing noises into the phone, then hangs up. I stare at her, totally shocked by what I just heard. "I didn't realize you had a kid," I say.

"Yes," she says. "He's 20 months old."

She doesn't offer me any more information, including his name, and her tone doesn't invite questions. But I realize if her kid is 20 months old, that means she had a baby when she was an intern. I look down at my abdomen and imagine what this would be like if I were pregnant right now. I shudder.

"What took you so long?" Alyssa asks me.

I don't dare tell her I was eating my dinner. I try to come up with something else reasonable I could have been doing. "Something came up with a patient," I lie.

"What?"

"Nothing important," I mumble.

Alyssa eyes the two bags of chips in my hands. She knows I'm lying, but thankfully, she doesn't press the matter further. That kid of hers is in for a rough childhood, that's all I've got to say.

"By the way," she says. "We've got to discuss your days off."

My heart leaps. All residents are required to get at least four days off per month. I say "at least" because you could potentially get more days off, but the chances of that are pretty small. Still, I'd been worried that Alyssa wasn't even planning on giving me my four days and that I'd just be working for 31 days straight.

She pulls out a calendar for the month. The options for days off are somewhat limited on our cycle of having overnight call every four days. We can't be off on our call days obviously, and the next day (the post-call days) are off-limits as well. The day after our post-call day, we have "short call" which means we can admit patients until 1 p.m. if it's a weekday. The next day is the "pre-call" day, which is the only day that can potentially be taken off.

Alyssa has circled all the pre-call days. Under some of them, she has written "Connie/Jane" and others she has written "Alyssa." I count the "Connie/Jane" days and see there are exactly four and exactly four "Alyssa" days. "These are your days off," she says.

I notice there's one day that's circled as a potential day off but hasn't been assigned to anyone. "What about that day?" I ask her. "That could be a day off, right?"

Alyssa glares at me. "You know, if you get an extra day off, that means that your resident and your attending have to do your work *for* you. Does that seem fair?"

I swallow and think of Alyssa cooing to her son on the phone. "Well, *you* could take the day off."

She hesitates a moment, as if she's almost considering it. I want her to take the day off. Not so much so that she could be with her son, but because right now, a day off from Alyssa seems almost as good as a day off from work. But then she shakes her head angrily. "No," she says. "It's more fair this way."

Your loss, Alyssa.

"Okay," she says, "let me tell you about your next patient."

I nod and grab for my notes from my white coat pocket. And that's when I realize that my notes are gone. All the notes and paperwork I have from the patients I've seen today and will be covering on call have inexplicably vanished. My stomach sinks.

"What are you waiting for?" Alyssa asks, glaring at me impatiently. She looks down at her watch.

I can't tell her that I lost all my notes. Not only do I need those notes to get through the call, but the notes have private patient information on them. Alyssa will murder me if I tell her I lost them. She will literally pick me up and toss me through the window like a rag doll.

So instead I clear my throat and force a smile.

"I just ran out of paper," I say.

I hop up and grab a yellowing paper from tray of the perpetually out-of-order printer and sit down across from Alyssa, poised to take notes as quickly as possible and then go find my lost papers.

"By the way," Alyssa says, "can I take a look at the med list on Chandler?"

Crap. Does she know? Can she read my mind?

"Um," I say. "I left it… in my locker."

Alyssa narrows her eyes. "Why on earth would you do that?"

I swallow. "So I wouldn't lose it."

Alyssa must smell blood, but she just shakes her head at me and doesn't press me further. Thank God.

As soon as Alyssa finishes telling me about the new patient, I am off like a rocket. My first stop is the cafeteria, where against all odds, Kali is still eating lunch. She has a nice life.

"Hey!" she says cheerfully. "Back for seconds?"

I wish. "Kali," I say. "When I was sitting here, did you notice if I had some white papers with me?"

"Oh sure," she says, grinning at me. "You don't forget a thing like that."

"This is serious," I say. I'm getting close to tears. "Those were all the notes on my patients and now I can't find them."

Kali is frustratingly unperturbed. "Well, just retrace your steps. Where have you been today?"

"Everywhere!" I cry. I really have. I've been to every unit of the hospital as well as to the Emergency Room.

"Well, where did you see them last?"

"I don't know!"

Kali wipes her mouth off with a napkin, and struggles to her feet. "Okay, come on. I'll help you look."

I have officially started to panic though. I keep thinking about all that patient information, open for anyone to find. Like Mr. Chandler's HIV status. I could go to *jail* for this. Although, in all honestly, jail might be slightly preferable to my current situation.

I'm already picturing how I'd look in an orange prison jumpsuit when I nearly collide with a janitor who is wheeling a large trash receptacle down the hallway. I look down into the trash and I can't even believe my eyes: it's my notes!

"That's mine!" I scream, pointing at the slightly soiled papers wedged between a banana peel and a bunch of crumpled up paper towels. I reach into the trash and carefully extract it with my thumb and fore-finger, trying my best not to touch anything else. The notes are stained but intact. "Where did you find it?"

The janitor looks from the papers to my face. "*En el cuarto del baño,*" he says.

I'm attempting to access my high school Spanish when Kali speaks up: "You left it in the bathroom."

Wow. I didn't even realize I'd been to the bathroom today.

Hours Awake: 12
Chance of doing something else dumb in the next 18 hours: 110%

13

I GET TWO MORE ADMISSIONS RIGHT IN A ROW AFTER that and hardly have a moment to breathe. There's one point at about 3 a.m. when I realize that I haven't used the bathroom in a good eight hours. On the plus side, that means I haven't had an opportunity to lose anything else in there. Anyway, there's no time for such frivolous things right now—the nurses are staring at me, all waiting for me to complete my latest admission orders.

"Can you page Dr. Reilly?" I hear one of the nurses say.

My head jerks up involuntarily. Sexy Surgeon hasn't been by to rescue me once tonight. But I don't miss him. I swear I don't.

Well, maybe a little.

"Good luck with that," another nurse says. "Dr. Reilly *never* answers his pager."

That statement is met with a smattering of giggles and agreement.

"True," the first nurse says. She's a matronly woman in her fifties. "He's cute though. I can put up with a lot if they're cute."

"Yeah, and he's *really* cute," a third nurse chimes in.

I can't help but feel annoyed. Mostly because I know that there's no level of cuteness that I, as a female (human), could obtain that would allow me to get away with treating the nurses like crap the way Ryan does.

I finish up my orders, hand them over to the nurse, and race down the hallway to the bathroom. I make it to the stall seconds before any loss of continence occurs. Good thing I've barely had time to drink anything tonight.

I'm pulling up my scrub pants, my elbow pressed against the stall door to keep it closed since none of the bathroom stalls have functional locks, when I hear the page booming from the loudspeakers overhead: "Dr. McGill, please call extension 3425!"

Okay, that's the unit I'd just been sitting on a minute earlier. I probably forgot to sign my orders again, but why would they page me overhead for something like that? I check my pager to make sure I didn't miss a page. I haven't. I quickly wash my hands and race out of the bathroom. It's got to be an emergency if they paged me overhead.

A nurse named Beth is waiting for me when I

arrive back on the unit. I double over for a moment, puffing unattractively.

"What's going on?" I gasp.

"Mr. Chandler asked for a higher dose of Benadryl," Beth says.

I stare at her. "You paged me overhead for *that*?"

Beth shrugs.

I am so tired. I feel like I'm going to cry. "This is an outrage! You can't even *pee* in this place!" I'm almost screaming at this point.

A resident in scrubs sitting in the nurse's station looks up at the sound of my outburst. Naturally, I had to express my frustration about peeing in front of Sexy Surgeon. He grins at me sexily.

"Sorry," I mumble.

"You gave him 25 mg of Benadryl," Beth says. "He says it's not working and he needs 50 mg. So another 25 mg."

"Okay, sure," I say.

I start hunting around for Chandler's chart so I can write the order. I can just feel Ryan's eyes watching me, but I try to ignore him best I can.

"I can't believe you're giving in to the drug addict," he says.

I turn around to glare at him. "It's *Benadryl*. Last I heard, that's not a narcotic."

Ryan stands up to join me at the chart rack. He's closer to me than he needs to be. "Let me guess," he says. "The guy has been getting tons of narcotics, and finally your attending or Alyssa made you cut back.

So instead, he starts asking you for Benadryl. Like, all the freaking time."

I frown. "How did you know that?"

"Because, young Medicine Intern," he says, "Benadryl potentiates the effects of narcotics. All the smart addicts know that."

I narrow my eyes. "And how do *you* know that?"

"Because I work at County Hospital," he says with a shrug.

He's wrong. He's so wrong. He has no idea what he's talking about. And I really wish he'd wipe that smug grin off his face.

"I'm right," he says.

"This guy is not a drug addict," I insist as I pull Chandler's chart off the rack. I'm prepared to give him all the Benadryl he wants, if only to spite Ryan.

Anyway, I'm 100% sure he's not a drug addict.

"Yeah? What's his diagnosis?"

"Shingles."

"How old?"

"36."

"HIV-positive?"

I feel my fingers ball into fists. "Yes, but not from drugs."

Ryan raises his eyebrows. "You've *got* to be kidding me. What sob story did he feed to you?"

"His fiancé was cheating on him," I say, sticking out my chin.

Ryan starts to laugh. "Oh boy, he must have been so happy when he laid eyes on you."

That is totally untrue. I mean, well, yes, he *did* look happy when he saw me come into his room in the ER. But that's just because I was his doctor and he was in pain and he knew I was going to help him. Not because he saw me as some naïve little intern who he could manipulate to get pain meds.

Right?

Crap.

"What room is he in?" Ryan says, looking down at the chart. Before I can answer, he reads it off. "423. Chandler. Got it."

My stomach seizes up as I watch Ryan stride down the hallway in the direction of Chandler's room. This is bad. I start to chase him down. "What are you doing?"

"I'm doing you a huge favor," he replies.

Oh no.

I can't seem to stop him though. He slows down in front of Chandler's room, and doesn't even bother to gown up. He pulls on a pair of gloves with a loud snap and strides into the darkened room. I follow a few steps behind, fumbling with the fabric of the yellow isolation gown which doesn't seem to want to unfold for me.

"Mr. Chandler?" I hear Ryan ask. "My name is Dr. Reilly."

Alex Chandler struggles to sit up in bed. He rubs his eyes and looks at Ryan. "Hi," he says. He doesn't seem thrilled.

"I want to make something really clear to you, Mr.

Chandler," Ryan says, his face impassive. "We are not drug dealers here. You are not getting *any* more pain meds while you're here. No morphine, no Dilaudid, no Demerol, nothing. No Benadryl either. You can have Tylenol—that's it. So I want you to quit bothering poor Dr. McGill here because it's not going to work."

Chandler stares at Ryan in surprise. "I'm… you know I have shingles, right?"

"And you're using it as an excuse to get high," Ryan says. "Nice job. But it's not going to work anymore."

Chandler looks from me to Ryan, finally deciding to address me: "Dr. McGill, I swear to you, I'm not—"

"Don't bother," Ryan cuts him off. "She's not the boss. She's just an intern."

My face burns. I want to tell Alex Chandler that I'm sorry, that I didn't tell Ryan to talk to him this way, but my lips feel frozen.

"I'm going to report you to the patient advocate," Chandler hisses at Ryan. "You can't talk to a patient this way, *Dr. Reilly*."

"Go ahead," Ryan snorts. "Maybe you'll get lucky and she won't bother to check how many times you've been to the ER this month looking for drugs. Or in the ERs of other nearby hospitals." He raises his eyebrows. "And maybe she'll be blind too and won't see the track marks on your arms."

Oh God. He's right. How did I not notice that?

Alex Chandler's face has turned very red. "That's... you... I'm not..."

"Read my lips," Ryan says, folding his arms across his chest. "No more drugs. Not here. You're done.

"Fine," Chandler says roughly. And then he does something really unexpected, which is that he rips his IV right out of his arm. Tape and all. It must have hurt, but he doesn't even flinch. "I'm leaving. I'm not going to be treated this way."

He swings his legs over the edge of the bed and stands up. He's a little shaky with his first step, but then it's obvious he's not going to fall.

He glares at me. "Thanks for ratting me out to your *boyfriend* over here. Really classy."

My mouth falls open. I don't even know what to say.

Chandler pushes past me, his shoulder jostling mine, and the last word I hear him say before he leaves is: "Bitch."

———

I CAN'T STOP SHAKING.

After I fill out the paperwork for Alex Chandler to leave the hospital AMA (Against Medical Advice), Ryan follows me to a quiet corner outside of the ward and sits with me while I replay what just happened over and over. I feel like a complete idiot. Chandler was manipulating me all along and I hadn't the slightest clue. I spent the whole day defending him like a fool.

"Don't feel bad," Ryan says. "It's your first week. It happens to everyone."

"Did it happen to you?"

He grins. "No. But I'm much meaner than you are."

I bury my face in my hands. "I'm terrible at this."

"Yeah," Ryan agrees. "But so is everyone."

"No, I'm the worst."

"I think you're underestimating how bad everyone else is."

I'm not sure this line of reasoning is making me feel any better.

"That guy's been doing this for years, I'll bet," Ryan says. "He's a nice-looking guy so he makes himself look clean-cut just so he can fool some good-hearted person like you. He's an expert at it. And this is only your first week."

"Yeah," I mumble.

"Listen," Ryan says. "Are you done for the night?"

I nod.

"Good." He stands up then holds out his hand to help me to my feet. Ryan's hand feels so warm and comforting in mine that I feel sad when I have to let go of it. "I'm going to walk you to your call room."

Hopefully, I don't end up in the wrong room again and have to make Alyssa's bed.

He presses the button for the elevator. He tugs

absently at the V-shaped collar of his blue scrub top and I again see that tantalizing bit of blond chest hair peeking through. I don't know if he notices me looking, but he gives me this smile that I can't quite read.

The elevator comes a minute later and we both step inside. I lean against the back corner, and Ryan presses the button for the seventh floor. As the doors slide shut, he looks at me, no longer smiling. I look at him. And before I know what's happening, he moves toward me and starts kissing me.

I feel his hands running up my back and into my neck and my hair as his lips press against mine and his tongue penetrates my mouth. The bristles of his golden five o'clock shadow graze my chin hard enough to cause pain, but I can't get enough of it. I know it's a cliché, but I feel myself melting against him. Sexy Surgeon knows how to kiss, that's for sure. For once, I love how slow the elevators in this hospital are.

I hear the ding of the elevator reaching its destination and the doors swing open. Ryan's hand closes around mine.

"Come on," he says.

My heart leaps. Even though we're at work, there are two very reasonable, private bedrooms for us to retire to. Not that I'm going to sleep with Ryan Reilly. Not in the literal or figurative sense of the word. But I definitely would love to make out with him for another hour or three.

The fates are against me though. As usual.

Ryan's pager goes off. And the guy who never, ever, *ever* answers his pager looks down at the number, and says, "Shit, I gotta go, Jane."

I almost cry. "Seriously?"

He sighs and rubs his face. "Yeah, I don't want to either, believe me. Get some sleep, okay?"

How the hell am I supposed to sleep after that just happened? But I say, "Okay."

"To be continued," he says, and slips back into the elevator just before the doors slam shut.

Hours awake: 21
Chance of sexy time in near future: 25%

14

TIREDNESS WINS OUT AS USUAL, HOWEVER, AND I DO manage to squeeze in a couple of hours of sleep before my pager wakes me around 7 a.m. I have another ten minutes left until my alarm goes off, but I figure at this point I better just get up. I make only a halfhearted attempt to look respectable by straightening out my ponytail, but I don't even bother with the finger brushing. Even though Alex Chandler left the hospital, I now have nine patients to see before we round with Dr. Westin, who we're meeting at 8 a.m. By Alyssa's logic of allowing thirty minutes per patient, I should have started rounding at 3:30 a.m. So I'm way behind right now.

By some miracle, I get everything done and arrive at Dr. Westin's office only a few minutes late. Naturally, everyone is already there, and Alyssa is looking at her watch with an annoyed expression on her face. I want to take her watch and flush it down the toilet.

But I can't because I don't have time to go to the bathroom anymore.

"Why didn't you page me when Alex Chandler left AMA?" Alyssa snaps at me the second I enter the room.

"I told the nurses to page you and let you know," I say.

"The nurses?" Her voice is dripping with contempt. "*You* should have called me. Yourself."

Okay, the truth is, I knew I should have called Alyssa and told her myself what happened. But it was three in the morning, I was already shaken about Chandler going off on me, and I didn't feel like getting screamed at on top of it. So I made the nurses do it. I mean, he was already gone. There was nothing we could do about it.

"Sorry," I say.

"You should have called me," Alyssa says. "If anything happens with a patient, you call me. You should know that by now."

"I understand," I say.

"She's right, Jen," Dr. Westin says. "Listen to Alyssa. She knows a lot."

I hate everyone in this room.

We get up to go round on all our patients. I feel like I'm in a bit of a daze, and half the time when Dr. Westin asks me a question, my answer is, "What?" At one point, he just shakes his head at me and says, "My, my, my." I can tell I'm not really impressing anyone here.

When we get to Mrs. Jefferson's room, her big toothy smile makes me feel better for about half a second, right before Alyssa lays into me right in front of her and everybody. "How much fluid did she put out last night?"

Because she has bad heart failure, we are monitoring Mrs. Jefferson's "ins and outs," meaning, we record everything she drinks ("ins") and everything she pees ("outs"). As much as I feel sorry for myself right now, I feel slightly more sorry for the nurse who has to keep track of how much pee Mrs. Jefferson makes.

I fumble through my notes. "Um… two liters? No… three liters?"

"Which is it, Jane? Two or three?"

I just stare down at my notes. At this point, anything I said would be a guess and she knows it.

"It's your job to know the patient's ins and outs," Alyssa says. "It's not my job. It's *your* job."

"Sorry," I say.

"My, my," Dr. Westin says.

As the rest of the team walks out of the room, Mrs. Jefferson says to me, "Hey, Jane?"

She's not supposed to call me by my first name, but I don't mind it right now. It's better than "Doctor" with the scare quotes.

"What is it?" I say.

"Don't you let them get to you," Mrs. Jefferson says. That puff of gray hair on her head makes her look very wise all of a sudden. "I know you're doing a good job, sweetie. You're a good doctor. And I know because I dealt with lots of doctors."

I nod.

"Don't worry," she says. "You're real sweet now, but in a year, you're going to be like a cougar. Just like that tall lady doctor who yelled at you. You'll see."

I can't help but laugh.

"One other thing," Mrs. Jefferson says. "Would you mind giving my husband a call, just to tell him what's going on with me? His number's in the front of the chart as my emergency contact."

"Sure," I say, putting it on my checklist to make sure it gets done. At least I can manage to not screw that up.

―――――

WE FINISH up with rounds and I find a quiet place to get my work done, and after a few minutes, Kali joins me. I have to admit, I look around for Ryan. I know that nothing is going to happen right this minute, me with a ton of paperwork to do and him with… I don't know, *surgery* to do. But I want to see him. Maybe sneak one more kiss in the elevator.

I hate myself for liking him so much.

I'm working my way through the long checklist of things I need to do before I can go home and go to sleep when an intern named Dave wanders over to us.

His brown hair is sticking straight up and he looks really freaked out.

"Hey," he says to me, running his hand through his hair, making it stick up even more. "Have you seen Connie?"

I shake my head. Connie is very focused on getting out of the hospital as fast as she can, which means when I see her, she's often just a blur.

"She signed out to me an hour ago," Dave says, "but then one of her admissions from last night got his third set of cardiac enzymes back and it was elevated. So… that means he's having a heart attack. Right?"

"Right," I say. "I think so."

I glance over at Kali, who shrugs.

"So I paged Connie to tell her and ask her what to do," Dave explains. "But she's not answering, so… I don't know what to do. What do I do?"

Kali and I exchange looks. "I think you're supposed to start the patient on a heparin drip?" Kali suggests.

"Maybe you should call cardiology?" I say.

Dave just stares at us.

And then I get this great idea. Connie has been Miss Perfect to this point. If I call Alyssa and tell her that Connie left the hospital before finding out if her patient was having a heart attack or not, that might deflect some of Alyssa's anger from me. That would be awesome.

Also, we could figure out how to treat the patient. That would be helpful too.

Dave stands by while I page Alyssa. She answers quickly, which is one thing I can definitely say about Alyssa: she is prompt. "Dr. Morgan, returning a page," she barks into the phone.

"Hi," I say. "It's Jane."

"What is it?" she asks, preemptively disgusted by anything I have to tell her.

"So Connie left about an hour ago," I say. "She signed out to the on-call intern. But now her patient ruled in for a heart attack. And she's not answering her pager. So…"

"So…?" Alyssa prompts me.

"So the intern isn't sure what to do," I say.

"And what did you tell him?"

"I told him I'd page you," I say lamely. Alyssa has no answer for that, so I add, "I mean, it's Connie's patient, not mine, so I don't really know him…"

"You don't?" Alyssa says. "Jane, didn't we round on *all* the patients this morning? This is why. So you know how to manage patients that aren't just your own and not just always ask me for help. What were you doing while we were discussing the plan for Connie's patients?"

I think I was half-asleep.

"Listening," I answer promptly.

"Then what would you like to do for the patient?" she asks me.

I bite my lip. I look over at Kali, who is miming

something I can't quite catch. It looks like she's telling me to go fishing. "Call cardiology?"

Alyssa sighs. "Let me talk to the on-call intern."

Gratefully, I hand the phone over to Dave. I shake my head at Kali.

"I can't believe this," I mutter. "Connie screws up and I'm the one who gets yelled at. What's wrong with her anyway? Why did she shut off her pager? Doesn't she have any sense of responsibility?"

Kali chews the back of her pen. I had already pegged her as a pen-chewer, so it's gratifying to see I'm right about at least one thing today.

"Don't take this the wrong way," Kali says, "but you need to watch out for Connie. Seriously."

"What does *that* mean?"

"Connie's got some evil in her," Kali says. "I mean, she's a *derm* resident."

In medicine, there is something known as the ROAD specialties, which is an acronym for the four specialties that have the best reimbursement to hours ratio. Basically, great lifestyle with lots of money. ROAD stands for:

Radiology

Ophthalmology

Anesthesiology

Dermatology

Naturally, it's competitive to land a residency in any of these lucrative specialties. But by far, the most competitive is dermatology because there are so few slots and the residency is especially cushy. You need the right combination of grades, board scores, letters of recommendation, and research. And medical students who want to end up as dermatologists will do anything to get there.

Even kill for it.

No, not really. They won't kill. But anything short of that is probably fair game. Like they might trip you pretty badly or stab you a little bit. They will do just about anything to make you look bad in front of the people grading you so that they end up with the higher grade. They are experts at brown-nosing and squeezing out the highest grade they possibly can.

For example, there was a guy in my class named Ned who wanted more than anything to do dermatology, even though on every rotation, he swore that was the specialty he was interested in. For example, when he was on OB/GYN, he wanted to be an obstetrician, on cardiology a cardiologist, etc. When I was rotating on pediatrics with him, Ned looked up all the labs on my patients as well as his, so if I was missing any piece of information, he immediately had it ready. Just to make me look bad. It worked really well.

"Connie doesn't seem that way to me," I say to Kali. "She's not competitive at all. She's actually kind of a slacker."

"Exactly!" Kali says, gesturing emphatically. "She's obviously really brilliant and good at getting what she wants. And now that she's landed the residency she wants, she's applying all that intelligence and focus into doing the absolute least amount of work possible. She's cutthroat about being a slacker."

I start to laugh. "Kali, that's kind of ridiculous."

"Ridiculous or absolutely on target?"

"No, ridiculous."

Kali shrugs. "Believe what you want. But just wait and see. The second you try to get Connie to do any real work, the claws are going to come out."

God, I really hope not. There are more claws out than I know what to do with right now.

I check my to-do list and remember that I need to call Mrs. Jefferson's husband. Considering this patient was the only person who's been nice to me in the last 24 hours, I feel like I ought to do it. I locate her chart at the nurse's station, and as promised, his phone number is listed under emergency contacts.

I dial the number and after several rings, I hear a male voice answer: "Hello?"

"Hello, is this…" I check the chart to read off his full name. "Is this… Thomas Jefferson?"

Seriously? Mrs. Jefferson's husband is named *Thomas Jefferson*? And now I'm really sorry I didn't check his name before calling because I have to clamp my hand over my mouth to keep from laughing.

"Yes, this is him," Thomas Jefferson says.

"This is Dr. McGill," I say. "I'm calling to give you an update on your wife Marquette."

Although what I really want to say is: *Your name is Thomas Jefferson! How did your parents give you that name? Are you aware of how funny this is?* I mean, I feel like he should at least acknowledge that, yes, he has the same name as our third president, and yes, it's weird. He should volunteer that information upon meeting any new person. Because obviously it's all we're going to be able to think about.

"Oh, thank you, Dr. McGill," Thomas Jefferson says. Then he writes the Declaration of Independence. (No, not really.)

"She's doing okay," I say. "She was having a little trouble breathing last night because of heart failure but we took off some fluid so she's doing better."

"It sounds like she's in real capable hands," Thomas Jefferson says. Then he makes the Louisiana Purchase. (No, not really.)

"Do you have any questions for me?" I ask him.

"No, I just appreciate you calling, sugar," Thomas Jefferson says. Then he funds the Lewis and Clark expedition. Okay, I need to stop this.

Thomas Jefferson actually seems like a really nice man, so I hang up the phone on a good note. I'm nearly done with my checklist, and I've made it through Call #2. I've been a doctor for a whole week, I haven't killed anyone, and I haven't even cried.

Yet.

———

THE DECISION of whether or not to take a nap post-call is a complicated one. Many factors go into this decision.

I hate taking naps. When I was a kid, I really hated it. I remember being forced to lie on the mat in kindergarten, my tiny fists clenched tightly at the indignity of it all. I never slept. I just find it hard to sleep in the middle of the day. I also find it completely disorienting to wake up from a nap.

If I don't sleep at all on call, such as during my last call, I pretty much am forced to take a nap, because I just feel too damn exhausted. But now I'm on the fence. I slept a solid three hours. I could probably make it till tonight without sleep. On the other hand, I am pretty tired.

Finally, I lie down in my bed and stare up at the ceiling, deciding to let my body dictate what it wants to do right now. After 30 hours of being in the hospital and having to bend to the whims of Alyssa, my pager, the nurses, and my patients, it feels decadent to just be able to do whatever I want right now.

A few minutes into my potential nap, my phone starts ringing. I check the number, hopeful it's someone I don't recognize. Really, I'm hoping it's Sexy Surgeon, having tracked down my number. But instead, it's the opposite of Sexy Surgeon: namely, my mother. I see the area code of her apartment in Queens and hesitate only a second before picking up.

I pick up. "Hi, Mom," I say.

"So how's it going?" she asks with breathless antic-ipation.

When I was young, my mother decided for me that I was going to be a doctor. The decision was not made lightly. She dropped out of college because she was getting married and hadn't been particularly good at school anyway. She was a housewife, then a stay-at-home-mom, then she came to realize that her husband was an alcoholic compulsive gambler who didn't particularly want to reform. They got divorced, he took off, and then she was left with a small child and not too many career options.

I can't remember a time in my childhood when my mother wasn't working at least two minimum-wage jobs. She was always shuttling me off to my grandparents for free babysitting because paying for a sitter was just out of the question. But when she took me to my pediatrician for my annual visits, she saw a woman who made a great living, was well respected, and in no position to have her entire life wrecked by a deadbeat husband.

And that's my secret. I didn't become a doctor because of some great love of medicine and healing. I did it mostly because my mother convinced me that it would be a secure, stable career. Don't tell the admis-sions committee at my med school.

"It's going… okay," I say cautiously.

"That's great," she says. "I'm so proud of you."

I bite my tongue. Mom and I had always been super close, which makes it hard to conceal from her my growing dissatisfaction with my career. That is, with the career *she picked for me*. I don't feel like an independent, intelligent, respected career woman. I feel exhausted, dumb, and mistreated.

And what really sucks is that while no man is in any position to destroy me financially, I've done a pretty good job of that myself. Thanks to college and med school, I am now a quarter of a million dollars in debt. Whenever I start to think about it, I feel a crushing weight on my chest. That's a lot of debt. It's going to dictate everything I do in life. I can never stay home with my kids because I've got to be working to pay back my debt. (Lucky for me, children are nowhere on my horizon right now.)

Sometimes I think I've made a huge mistake with my career and it's all her fault.

"Did you get to save anyone's life yet?" Mom asks.

I can't help but think back to my one Code Blue, and how I spent the whole time cleaning up the mess from my popsicle. "Not really."

"It's just so exciting," Mom sighs. "You're going to have such a great life, sweetie. You'll see. You made the right decision going to med school."

Right now, I'm just having a lot of trouble believing that something making me so suffocatingly miserable was really the right decision.

15

SHORT CALL

THE NEXT DAY, I'M ON SHORT CALL, MEANING OUR team takes new admissions until 1 p.m. at a maximum of two patients per intern. It means we can sleep in our own beds, but it's still a rough day. Especially since we're expected to meet Dr. Westin to round at 7 a.m. in order to leave time for everything else we have to do.

Since we're meeting at 7a.m., I'm expected to have pre-rounded on all my patients prior to that. I have eight patients, so at Alyssa's estimate of thirty minutes per patient, I should rightfully be showing up at 3 a.m. That is not going to happen. Instead, I come in at 6 a.m.

The first patient I go see is Mrs. Coughlin. Her biopsy came back, and it seems like her tumor is most likely pancreatic cancer. Pancreatic cancer is Bad Cancer. Not that any kind of cancer is good cancer, but pancreatic cancer has an especially poor prognosis. Dr. Westin broke the news to her, and I hid, because I was too scared to see her reaction.

Now oncology and surgery have decided that her best bet is a Whipple procedure, also known as a pancreaticoduodenectomy (say that ten times fast). Basically, it involves removal of part of the stomach, the pancreas, the small intestines, and the complete removal of the gallbladder. The surgery team is going to be responsible for getting consent, and then she'll leave our service and they'll take over her care.

"I'm going to have nothing left inside me!" Mrs. Coughlin says to me, but she smiles like she made a joke. She doesn't seem as scared as I might have expected. Right now, she's calmly knitting.

"You'll have a few things left," I say.

"Well, I hope so," Mrs. Coughlin says.

"Someone from Surgery will come by to get consent," I tell her.

"Oh, he already did," she says. "Very early this morning. Dr. Reilly, he said his name was."

Sexy Surgeon again. Sometimes I'm beginning to wonder if there are any other surgery residents in the whole hospital.

"That Dr. Reilly is so handsome!" Mrs. Coughlin says, clutching her chest. "Do you know him, Dr. McGill?"

"Sort of," I mumble.

"And he's single," she says. She points to her left hand. "No ring. I told him he should ask you out."

I groan. "Thanks."

Mrs. Coughlin continues to gush about the handsome Dr. Reilly for several more minutes, until I finally interrupt her to listen to her heart and lungs. This is not my favorite way to start the day.

I just barely get through my work and am racing to Dr. Westin's office, determined to be on time. Of course, I'll never be earlier than Connie. She only has one patient again, somehow.

Connie has already finished discussing her one patient, so I start in on my huge list. It takes forever, because Alyssa won't let me get one word out without interrupting me. I feel like I'm on trial, being cross-examined on the witness stand. "How come you didn't mention the drop in Mrs. Jefferson's hematocrit?" she demands to know.

"Uh…" I fumble through my notes to find Mrs. Jefferson's most recent labs. Her hematocrit was 34 yesterday. Now it's 32. "It only dropped two points."

"She's already in heart failure," Alyssa says. "Do you really want to put more stress on her heart?"

"So…" I search Alyssa's face, trying to figure out what she wants me to do. "Should we transfuse her?"

"Transfuse her!" Alyssa looks at me in horror. "Jane, you can't be serious."

No, I was just kidding. Ha ha.

"Um," is what I actually say.

"Why don't you start by doing a guaiac," Alyssa sighs.

Medical jargon:

"Doing a guaiac": Stick your finger in the patient's

rectum so you get some poop on your finger, smear the poop on a special card, and see if it changes color when you put a special solution on it, which would indicate the presence of blood.

"Okay," I say.

Alyssa eyes me critically. "You really need to read more, Jane."

It takes me so long to get through all my patients that Dr. Westin actually feels a need to comment on the size of my service. It's a bit of vindication.

"You're treating half the hospital, aren't you, Jan?" he says. And he's getting ever closer to my real name too—only one letter left to go. Score!

I shrug modestly.

"Interns are capped at 12 patients, aren't they?" Dr. Westin asks Alyssa.

"Yes," Alyssa confirms.

"I think we better try to even things out a bit on this short call," he says. "Jan, you can take one patient. Connie, you can admit three."

Connie's eyes widen for a moment, but she doesn't say anything.

"That would really help," I speak up gratefully. It's actually the first nice thing anyone on my team has done for me, although it's probably more because he's worried I'll hit my cap and not be able to take any more patients.

Still, it will be a huge relief to do only one admission today. My to-do list is already about ten times longer than Connie's and it would be nice to get out of here sometime tonight.

The first place I go after I leave Dr. Westin's office is to Mrs. Jefferson's room. I figure I may as well get the worst of it over with first. Mrs. Jefferson is sitting in bed, reading a magazine, flipping the pages with her chubby fingers. Her gray hair is all poofed out as usual, but now it's covered in little sparkly clips. The clips don't seem to be controlling her hair in any way and appear to be merely decorative.

"Well, hello, Dr. Jane," Mrs. Jefferson says, her face beaming with a big smile. "Come to visit me again, did you?"

"Hi, Mrs. Jefferson," I say.

"Oh, didn't I tell you to please call me Marquette?"

I nod, unable to bring myself to tell her about the rectal exam. "I like your clips."

Mrs. Jefferson pats her head and laughs. "My grand-daughter gave me these, so I got to wear them." Her eyes light up. "Do you want to see photos of my grandkids?"

I don't really, if I'm being entirely honest. I've got a ton of work to do. But I feign enthusiasm as Mrs. Jefferson fishes out her phone and shows me about two thousand photos of her grandkids doing every conceivable activity. She's even got several of them on the toilet. Speaking of which…

"Mrs. Jefferson," I say. "I've got to do a rectal exam."

"Okay," she says without batting an eye. Then she adds, "I'm sorry."

"No, *I'm* sorry," I say.

"Oh, honey," Mrs. Jefferson says. "Don't you worry about me. I'm used to it."

I decide that Mrs. Jefferson has enough strength to turn herself with my help, so I don't need to drag a nurse into the room. She grabs the bedrail and turns herself onto her side, while I spread her butt cheeks with my gloved hands.

Sometimes I really, *really* don't like being a doctor.

Her buttocks are so large that I really can't see anything. I fish around with my lubed finger, and I start to worry that my fingers literally are not long enough to reach her rectum. But then I find it, although not before Mrs. Jefferson laughs and says, "Don't fall in!"

I'm sweating like a pig by the time I extract my right hand, carefully holding out my index finger to preserve the specimen. I reach into my white coat pocket with my clean hand to pull out a guaiac card and…

Oh no, where *is* it?

I've got a lot of junk in my pocket, but I'm sure I had a guaiac card in there. Still holding my poop-smeared right index finger in the air, I use my left hand to start emptying the contents of my pocket. I've built a three-inch high pile of crumpled papers, pens, sticky notes, and gauze on Mrs. Jefferson's night-table by the time it becomes obvious that I do not have a guaiac card in my pocket.

Shit.

(Literally.)

"I'll be right back," I tell Mrs. Jefferson.

I walk into the hallway, my right index finger still stuck up in the air. I cannot believe this is happening. How could I have done a rectal exam without double-checking to make sure I was prepared? Now I have to walk around with poop on my finger, looking for a guaiac card. I'm not even sure where they are on this floor.

"June!"

I look up and am horrified to see Dr. Westin grinning down at me. I have no idea what he's doing on the wards. Attendings never show up on the wards—it would be like God coming down from heaven and just, like, hanging out at the mall. And of course, the one time he chooses to do it, I've got poop all over my finger.

"Hello, Dr. Westin," I say politely, trying my best not to let my finger get contaminated. Or more accurately, not to let my finger contaminate something else.

"Is everything going all right?" he asks me.

"Great," I say through my teeth. My finger is starting to ache, but there's no way I'm going to tell him the dumb thing I just did. He'll probably tell Alyssa and then I'll never hear the end of it.

"I know intern year can be tough," Dr. Westin says.

"Yes," I say. Is he done?

"Very tough," he says. "Did I ever tell you about the time when…"

I keep a smile plastered across my face as Dr. Westin recounts the story of his first call as an intern. I swear to God, this is the longest story in the history of the world. Why won't he leave me alone? Why does he have to choose this exact moment to take me under his wing?

"…and I've never been able to eat meatballs again after that," Dr. Westin concludes, chuckling at his own joke.

"I'll bet," I say. Somebody shoot me.

"Well, I'll leave you to it then, June," Dr. Westin says. "You look like you're in the middle of something important."

No, I just have crap smeared all over my finger.

The second Dr. Westin disappears down the hall, I burst into the supply room. Keeping my finger elevated, I check every single drawer and shelf using my left hand. There is not one guaiac card in sight. This is unbelievable. Where are those goddamn cards?

Does poop expire? Do I have a time limit to get this crap smeared on a card before the results will be invalidated? God, I hope not.

Finally, I suck up my self-respect and approach one of the nurses, a tiny blonde named Angie.

"Hi," I say. "I was wondering if you knew where the guaiac cards are?"

Angie looks me over, from my rumpled white coat and scrubs, to my gloved right hand with my finger still stuck straight up in the air. Then she bursts out laughing.

"Oh, Doctor," she giggles. "You've got to go into the room *prepared*."

"Yeah," I mumble. "I'll keep that in mind next time. So, um, do you know where…?"

"I'll grab one for you," she says.

I stand at the nurse's station, my blood pressure rising slightly when another nurse hijacks Angie on the way to get the card, forcing me to spend extra time waiting with poop on my finger. But finally she returns with about half a dozen guaiac cards and even a small bottle of developing fluid. "You can keep this," she tells me, waggling the fluid bottle in my face.

"Thank you," I say.

"That will make you *very* popular," she says.

"I know," I say. And I'm not even joking. Guaiac developing fluid is a scarce commodity.

I smear the card, and practically rip off my glove with relief. I put a drop of fluid on the smear and wait.

It's negative.

I guess it's good news for Mrs. Jefferson, but I'm a little peeved that I had to run around with poop on my finger for nothing. Not that I expected any other outcome.

I'm finding a trash to toss the contaminated card, when all of a sudden, I'm face to face with Connie. I'm pretty sure her one patient isn't on this floor, so I don't know what she's doing here.

I can't help but notice that Connie hasn't dressed in scrubs today, but instead is wearing a fitted white blouse with a beige skirt, and knee-high boots. Knee-high boots has never been a look I could pull off. I always feel vaguely like an unhip cowboy.

"Can I talk to you for a minute, Jane?" Connie says to me.

"Sure," I say. I locate a trash and toss the guaiac card inside. "What's up?"

Unlike me, Connie isn't wearing her hair in a ponytail, so she tosses her long, dark locks back behind her shoulders. She's actually very pretty. Her best feature may be her skin, which is completely flawless. Why do all dermatologists have such great skin?

"I wanted to talk to you about the distribution of patients today," she says.

"Oh?"

She nods. "I just… I think it's a little unfair."

I'm guessing she doesn't think it's unfair that I have eight patients and she has one. I suspect the unfair part is how there's a tiny chance she'll have to do more work than me today.

"You think so?" I say.

"I mean, an admission is a lot of work," Connie points out. "You already know all your eight patients, but it's going to take me forever to get through three admissions."

"Well, I think Dr. Westin is worried about me going over the cap," I say.

"Yes, but isn't Mrs. Coughlin being transferred to surgery soon?" she reminds me. "Plus you have a couple of other possible discharges for tomorrow, right?"

I set my jaw. I know what she's doing and I don't want to let her do it. The attending decreed that she's got to take three admissions today. And damn it, she's going to do it! "Not that many discharges," I say.

"Yeah, but if I take these three patients, I'll have four," she says. "And if you have three of yours go home tomorrow in addition to Mrs. Jefferson, you'll only have five. I mean, what's the difference if you have one more than that? You definitely won't hit the cap."

"Well, not necessarily…" I say.

No! I will not give in!

Connie studies my face for a moment. "Jane," she says. "You seem really unhappy."

I look at her in surprise. Well, yeah, I'm unhappy. I'm an intern. But I didn't know I was so visibly, notably unhappy that other people would feel compelled to comment. "Well, I mean, it's been a rough week…"

"You just don't have a very good attitude," she says. "I think that's the problem."

Oh, is *that* the problem?

"I was really looking forward to this year," Connie says sadly. "I really wanted to learn as much as I could. And I feel like your bad attitude is just… it's *ruining* it for me."

My jaw falls open. I'm *ruining* her intern year? Is that really what she's accusing me of? I don't even know what to say. I want to tell her she's full of shit (much like my finger used to be), but the truth is, I feel a little guilty. I hate the idea that I might be making everyone around me unhappy.

"So what are you saying?" I ask her.

"I'm saying you should do your fair share of the work," Connie says, folding her hands across her chest. She's wearing red nail polish, and unlike me, her fingernails aren't bitten to shreds.

"It's not even my decision," I say. "Dr. Westin was the one who made the decision. This is what *he* wants."

Connie raises her eyebrows at me. "Only because you complained this morning."

I did?

"I talked to Alyssa about it," Connie says. "She said if you agreed, we'd split today's admissions evenly, two each. That would be more fair."

My cheeks burn. If I made a similar request of Alyssa, she'd have given me the glowering of a life-time. But she could never say no to Connie, naturally.

I know I promised myself I would say no, but I don't want Connie going around telling everyone that I'm not a team player. I *am* a team player. Also, I'm apparently a pushover. "Fine," I say. "We can split the admissions."

"Fine," Connie says. The bitch doesn't even say *thank you*.

And somehow, I don't know how, I end up doing two admissions while Connie does one.

16

IT'S NEARLY 7 P.M. BY THE TIME I LEAVE THE hospital. I try not to think about the fact that I've spent 13 straight hours at the hospital, and focus more on which spectacular TV dinner I'm going to eat when I get back to my room. I also fantasize a lot about my bed.

Back in my suite, I shove a package of frozen fettuccine alfredo into the microwave then hit the bathroom to wash the hospital off my hands. Except before I make it into the bathroom, I find something taped to the bathroom door. It's five pages long and I'm pretty sure it's from Julia. I rip it off the wall.

The first page is a schedule of when each of us has to clean the bathroom. Okay, fair enough. It says: Jane—Tuesdays and Saturdays, Julia—Thursdays and Sundays. And then a list of major holidays and who will be cleaning the bathroom during each of these holidays. So... does this mean we're cleaning the bathroom *four times a week*? Is she kidding me? It's a tiny bathroom and the only people who use it are the two of us. How does it require such frequent cleaning? And when exactly am I supposed to do this cleaning, considering I practically live in the hospital?

The next three pages are detailed instructions on how to clean the bathroom.

The final page is a photocopy of the receipt from a local drug store for cleaning supplies. She spent $89.34 on bathroom cleaning supplies. Why do we need "bleach foamer"? And why are all our cleaning supplies "organic"? It's not like we're going to *eat* them.

At the bottom of the receipt, Julia has written my share: $44.67. That's seriously more than my food budget for the month. She has *got* to be kidding me. I make minimum wage. (Although admittedly, minimum wage is somewhat lucrative when you're working like a billion hours a week.)

I am not paying for her stupid organic cleaning supplies. No way. No way in hell.

Oh, who am I fooling? I am definitely going to end up paying her.

———

AT SOME POINT, I start watching television in my bedroom and drift off. What ends up waking me is a pounding noise at the door to the suite. Rubbing my eyes, I stumble in the direction of the door and fling it open without even asking who it is. As soon as I see who's standing there, my eyes fly open and I'm instantly awake.

It's Sexy Surgeon.

"Hey," he says. He's wearing his scrubs, which I think is the only outfit I've ever seen him in. Lucky thing he looks so good in them. He squints at my face. "Did I wake you up?"

"A little," I admit.

It occurs to me at that moment that Julia is going to throw a fit if she realizes he's at the door. The fact that she's not complaining at this very moment is evidence that she's not here. But she's probably got hidden cameras installed somewhere. Or at the very least, a spy situated in the hallway. Maybe there's a sniper out here, who's ready to pick Ryan off at any second.

I grab his arm. "Get in here, quick," I say.

He looks at me in surprise, but follows me inside. I don't let go of his arm until we're safely inside my bedroom with the door shut.

"Okay," I say, letting out a breath. "We're safe."

Ryan raises his eyebrows. "We weren't safe out there?"

"My roommate," I explain, waving my finger in a circle to demonstrate Julia's loony behavior.

"Gotcha," Ryan says. He grins at me. "Nice room."

"Thanks."

"I like the skeleton," he says.

"Thanks."

He grins wider. "He's not going to get jealous and start haunting me, is he?"

I roll my eyes. "No."

"Because I know intern year can get pretty lonely so I wouldn't blame you if you and Skelly over there… well, you know…" He winks.

I put my hands on my hips. "Did you come here to make fun of me?"

That wipes the smile off his face. "No," he says. "I didn't."

He bridges the two-foot gap between him and me. He lowers his lips onto mine, and now we're kissing, and there are no pagers to go off, elevator doors to open, or anything to keep this from happening. We fall onto my bed and he gently pushes me down against the pillows, then climbs on top of me.

"You're so sexy, Jane," he breathes in my ear. And I almost believe him.

At first, I'm scared this is going to go further than I want it to (I just met him a week ago!), but he's actually very respectful.

Surprisingly respectful.

What he does with his lips on mine is very intense, but he doesn't make any move to push me further than that. His hands move up and down my chest and my thighs, but he doesn't try to get up my shirt or down my pants. His lips stay mostly on mine, although they make little excursions to my earlobes and that extra-sensitive area at the base of my neck.

We make out like the ship is going down, like we can't get enough of each other, but after an hour or so, the kisses become less hungry and more gentle, and we're cuddling more than kissing. I wouldn't have taken Sexy Surgeon for a cuddler. He just seems too busy. But it's nice to lie in his arms like we have all the time in the world, feeling the warmth and comfort of his body against mine. I could lie here forever.

"I've got to go," he says, as if on cue.

"Now?"

"I'm on call, actually," he says. He fishes into his pocket and retrieves his pager, which he's apparently been concealing from me.

I stare at him. "Seriously?"

He shrugs. "I've got an intern. He's handling most of it. But I told him I'd meet him in the ER..." He checks his watch. "About fifteen minutes ago."

"Seriously?"

He shrugs again. "Let him wait. He's just an intern."

"Thanks a lot."

Ryan grins, then he pulls away from me and adjusts the drawstring on his scrubs. "I'm going to hit the bathroom, then I'll leave."

My breath catches in my throat. "No! You can't."

"I can't leave?"

"No, I mean, you can't use the bathroom."

Ryan stares at me like I've lost my mind.

I blush. "My roommate is super weird about the bathroom. Can't you just use it at the hospital?"

He rolls his eyes. "Come on, Jane. Just let me go pee."

I'd like to let him—I really would. But the consequences of that could be dire. I show him Julia's Bathroom Manifesto. "Look what she put on the door!"

He takes the pages from me, and laughs as he flips through. "Whoa, you weren't kidding. She's nuts."

"See?"

"I'm still going to use the bathroom though," he says. He cuts off my protests with a kiss. "We're going to live dangerously for a change."

Our compromise is that he goes to the bathroom and I stand guard outside. He insists I'm being just as crazy as Julia, but I swear, he hasn't seen that evil glint in her eyes. If I'm going to be sleeping in the same apartment as her, I need to protect myself.

17

CALL #3

My first admission of the day is pregnant.

On the Medicine service, we're not supposed to admit pregnant patients. They're supposed to go to OB/GYN. But this one is okay. Mostly because it's a man. And he's pregnant not with a fetus but with a lot of fluid that can't get through his liver because his liver is hard as a rock thanks to years of drinking.

He really looks pregnant though.

His name is Jorge Sanchez and his belly is tense with fluid. His belly button has gone from innie to outie. His testicles are *huge*—I'm talking elephant testicles here. The plan is for me and Alyssa to drain the fluid in his belly then make sure it isn't infected. I'm supposed to be telling him about this.

Except like every other patient at County Hospital, he speaks no English.

So I'm standing in Mr. Sanchez's room, waiting for the translator phone to come through for me with someone who speaks Spanish. The phone is sitting on Mr. Sanchez's night table, the speakerphone filling the room with the music of Taylor Swift, the same song over and over. I am starting to believe that we are never, ever, ever going to get that translator on the phone. I have literally been waiting for ten minutes, just standing here and twiddling my thumbs.

Every once in a while, I try to ask Mr. Sanchez a question. I did, after all, take four years of Spanish in high school. Someone told me that Spanish would be a useful language to know, which it definitely would be, if I could actually remember more than a handful of words.

"*Uno momento mas*," I say to Mr. Sanchez.

"*No me importa esperar*," he says.

"Huh?" I say.

This translator better come through soon. Alyssa is supposed to meet me here in five minutes to do a paracentesis with me, meaning we'll remove his belly fluid. If I don't have consent from him by then, I don't know what she'll do to me and I'm scared to find out. I'm sure Connie would have had the translator on the phone five minutes ago. Connie probably would have taught Mr. Sanchez English by now.

"*Puedo tener un vaso de agua?*" Mr. Sanchez asks.

"Huh?" I say. How do you say "slower" in Spanish?

He tries saying it slower but I still have no idea what he's saying. How do you say "this totally blows" in Spanish?

A heavily-accented voice comes out of the speakerphone: "Hello?"

"Hello!" I say. "Are you the translator?"

"Yes, I am," the voice confirms.

I lunge forward excitedly, in an attempt to get closer to the phone. Unfortunately, in my eagerness, I trip over a wire. The phone goes crashing to the ground. I stare at it for a horrified second before scooping it up off the floor. "Hello? Hello?" I cry into the receiver.

I lost the connection.

This is one of those moments where you can do one of two things:

1. Burst into tears, shaking fist at the heavens, and yell out, "Nooooooo!!!!!!!"
2. Laugh.

Somehow, against all odds, I start to laugh. I cover my mouth with my hand so that Mr. Sanchez doesn't see and I attempt to stifle my snickers. It's not funny. But I guess it sort of is. In a really horrible kind of way.

At that moment, Alyssa pokes her head into the room. "Jane," she says. "Did you get the consent done yet?"

Screw this. I don't need a translator to get consent. "Give me a minute," I say.

I take the consent out of my pocket and put it down in front of Mr. Sanchez. "Es una consenta," I explain. "Necesita… um, sign. Sign-a." I make a motion like I'm signing a form. "Necesita put una needle in su estomago. Por la agua in su estomago." I pantomime fluid gushing out of the stomach. "Um, comprende?"

Mr. Sanchez looks up at me, then down at the paper. I have no idea if he had any clue what I just said, but he signs the consent anyway. Thank you, Mr. Sanchez!

I come out of the room, holding the consent up like a medal. Alyssa seems unimpressed by my ability to obtain a signature. "Did you get the supplies?" she asks.

"Um. No."

She sighs. "Okay, go get them."

I stare at her. "What supplies do we need?"

Alyssa raises her eyebrows. "Really, Jane. Come on, you should know this by now."

I should? I've been an intern less than two weeks. This is my first peritoneal tap. Why should I know this?

When it becomes obvious that I'm not going to magically know what supplies are needed for the tap, Alyssa starts ticking off what I need to get: "We need a red top tube, a purple top tube, a 25 gauge needle, a 20 gauge needle…"

I scramble to write everything down, knowing I'll get my ass handed to me if I forget a single item. I run to the supply room, and stock up on two of every-thing, figuring I'm sure to mess up at least once. I return to Mr. Sanchez's room, my arms brimming with supplies. Alyssa looks over the contents of my arms, probably secretly hoping I've forgotten something. I haven't.

"All right," Alyssa says. "I guess we can start." She eyes my face. "If we're worried about peritonitis, how many PMNs are we looking for in the tap?"

Say what? I have no idea what she's talking about, and I don't even know what the order of magnitude should be for the answer. Finally, I take a wild guess: "A hundred thousand?"

Alyssa couldn't look more shocked. "Are you kidding me?"

I try again: "Ten thousand?"

Alyssa gets these little pink spots on both her cheeks. "How could you do a paracentesis without knowing the number of PMNs diagnostic of peritonitis?"

It's probably a rhetorical question but I feel compelled to answer: "I figured I'd look it up after?"

Alyssa's lips become a thin, red line. "Go find out right now. Don't come back before you can tell me the answer."

Cursing to myself, I run out of the room to figure out the answer to the question. I don't want to miss the entire tap, so I've got to get an answer fast. Luckily, I see Connie at the other end of the hallway. Connie did a paracentesis a few days ago, so she surely knows the answer. Hopefully, she doesn't hate me so much that she'll refuse to tell me.

I race down the hall, yelling, "Connie!" She turns and her face sours considerably when she sees it's me. "Hey, I have a question."

"What is it?" Connie asks impatiently, doing an excellent impression of Alyssa.

"You did a paracentesis, right?"

Connie nods warily.

"Okay, so how many PMNs is the cut-off for peritonitis?"

I'm holding my breath. Connie shrugs. "I don't know. My patient didn't have peritonitis."

"But how do you know he didn't if you don't know the cut-off?"

Connie gives me a dirty look. It's becoming clear that she has no idea what the answer to the question is and also that this conversation isn't going in a positive direction. Luckily, Kali walks by at that moment. Kali, my savior.

"Kali!" I say. "Do you have a second?"

She holds her index finger and thumb about a millimeter apart. "I've got this long. What's up?"

"Have you done a paracentesis?"

Kali nods.

"Great!" I say. "So how many PMNs is the cut-off for peritonitis?"

And guess what? She has no idea. Neither do the next three interns that pass by. Yet somehow nobody but me has been thrown out of the room for not knowing.

Finally, I give in and go to a computer to look it

up. The computers have a ridiculously slow internet connection, but I finally find out from Wikipedia that the answer is 250. (I'm embarrassed that I wasn't even remotely close in my guesses.)

I return to Mr. Sanchez's room, armed with my answer. "Two-hundred-and-fifty!" I gasp heroically as I burst into the room.

"Right," Alyssa says.

She places a Band-Aid over the puncture site on Mr. Sanchez's belly. I can't even believe it. I missed the whole goddamn thing. She threw me out of the room for *nothing*, and I missed out on my procedure. This is so, so unfair.

Alyssa is not going to get away with it. Not this time.

Hours Awake: 5
Chance of Alyssa getting what's coming to her:
Like 5%?

18

Part of me is hoping Dr. Westin won't be around when I get to his office. I don't know exactly what I hope to achieve by coming here, but I feel like Alyssa's behavior has crossed some sort of line. I need to talk to a "grown up" about it.

The door to Dr. Westin's office is open in a welcoming way. As he sees me in the entranceway, he immediately waves to me enthusiastically. "Hi, Jill!"

Dr. Westin is nice. Even though he never gets my name right.

I stick my head inside the office. "Hey," I say. "Is it okay if I talk to you about something?"

"Of course!" He turns away from his computer and places his hands on his desk. Even though he's too thin and his hairline is receding, at least half a dozen female patients have referred to Dr. Westin as "that handsome doctor." At first, I couldn't even figure out who they meant. Recently, I've developed a theory that every male doctor who isn't outright disgusting with a huge hump on their back or something is seen as "handsome" by the general female population. This seems grossly unfair, but it's the least of my problems right now.

"Please, have a seat," he invites me.

I gingerly take a seat in front of his desk, like I'm worried Alyssa might suddenly pop out from a hidden corner. I momentarily get distracted by a framed photo on his desk of an athletic-looking brunette with a young boy who is a miniature version of Dr. Westin.

"It's about Alyssa," I begin.

Dr. Westin raises his eyebrows. "Yes…?"

"We don't really…" I take a breath. "Get along."

"My, my…" Dr. Westin looks very troubled. A deep crease appears in his brow.

"I feel like I can't ask her any questions," I say. "She's always angry at me. She makes me feel like I'm doing an awful job all the time. She never gives me any positive feedback. I just feel like… I can't function this way."

"My, my," he murmurs again. "And have you told this to Alyssa?"

I shake my head.

"Let me tell you a story, Jem," he says. Jem? He thinks my name is Jem? Wasn't that a cartoon rocker from the eighties? "Say there's this professor who notices that one of her students, Stacey, shows up for class ten minutes late one day. The professor thinks to herself that Stacey doesn't care at all about the class and she doesn't even have the courtesy to be on time. The professor thinks Stacey's interrupting the whole lecture, and that Stacey is overall just very inconsiderate."

"Uh huh," I say.

"Except here's what really happened," he goes on. "Stacey's grandmother was very ill and she went to see her over the weekend. Because the professor's class was so very important to her, she caught an early flight back to school in order to be sure to make it in time. Except the flight was delayed. Stacey caught a taxi straight to the school from the airport, all just so she could make it to that lecture."

"I see," I say, even though I think that Stacey and the professor both kind of seem like losers.

"Stacey and her professor needed to communicate," Dr. Westin says. "And that's what you and Alyssa need to do as well. You need to tell her how you feel."

I don't want to tell Alyssa how I feel. I just want to throw something at her.

"Can you do that for me, Jem?" he presses me.

"Okay," I finally say.

Dr. Westin rubs his hands together. "Good, good." He grins, showing a row of slightly yellowing teeth. "I predict that by the end of this rotation, you and Alyssa are going to be best friends."

Best friends. Yeah, maybe if we don't kill each other first.

As I'm rounding the corner to get to the cafeteria, I hear shouting. Female shouting. Not that yells and screams are an unusual occurrence in the hospital, but this sounds a little different somehow and the voices are oddly familiar. I slow to a stop and start searching for the source of what seems to be a really passionate fight.

After a minute, I find Kali and Julia standing in a nook by the staircase, glaring at each other. Julia is pointing a finger menacingly in Kali's direction. I'm actually a little frightened for Kali, who is half a head shorter.

"You think I don't know what you're doing?" Julia hisses.

"I have no idea what you're talking about," Kali says, although I can see a crease between her brows.

"You're sneaking out during your calls," Julia snaps. "I know it and soon our attending is going to know it."

"That's a complete lie," Kali lies.

My Dansko clogs squeak against the floor and both girls look up. I blush and wave awkwardly. "Hi," I say as I waggle my fingers. "Um, anyone want to get lunch?"

Julia looks from Kali to me with utter disgust. "Neither of you has any integrity," she says. She shifts her menacing finger to point in my direction. "I know you had a *boy* over the night before last," she says.

"Don't be silly," I say. I let out a little strangled laugh.

"He left the toilet seat up," Julia says.

Damn you, Sexy Surgeon! "I always pee with the toilet seat up," I lie.

Julia just shakes her head at me. She turns back to Kali. "If you do it again," she says, "you are going to suffer the consequences."

On those words, Julia turns on her heel and storms off in the opposite direction, leaving Kali and I with equally stunned expressions on our faces.

"Christ," Kali says. "How do you live with that crazy person? Aren't you afraid she'll murder you in your sleep?"

"A little," I admit.

"*If you do it again, you are going to suffer the consequences*," Kali says in a mockingly high voice. "Who the hell does she think she is? A Super-Villain? I'm just giving shots to my diabetic cat. Sheesh."

"Yeah, well, wait until you hear what she left on the bathroom door." I quickly get Kali up to date on Julia's Bathroom Manifesto, and the fact that I found a Kitchen Manifesto this morning taped to the refrigerator. I fear that I'm going to be spending most of my intern year cleaning the bathroom and kitchen of our apartment.

"Wow," Kali breathes. "What a nut job." She links arms with me and starts pulling me in the direction of the cafeteria. "But what I really want to know is, who is this *boy* you had over the other night, Dr. McGill?"

My cheeks grow hot. I'm not sure if I want to share this with anyone, even Kali, who is quickly becoming my best friend around here.

"You're blushing!" Kali says joyfully. "You can't deny it now because you're blushing. Spill!"

"It's just a surgery resident I met in the hospital," I mumble.

Kali stops and examines my face. "Wow, you really like him. You're *in love*."

"Oh my God, I am not in love!" I'm really not. "I hardly know him. Actually, he's kind of a jerk."

"No, you're in love," Kali insists gleefully. "You luuurve him! You lurve him and you want to have like a million of his babies."

I cringe. "Don't mention having babies. Please."

Kali sighs, suddenly glum. "You've got a cute surgeon and all I've got is a diabetic cat."

"I think I would take your cat over the surgeon," I say. "Really."

"Well," Kali says thoughtfully. "He *is* a very sweet cat." She brightens. "Do you want to see some new photos?"

I really, really don't. "Sure," I say. Apparently, I am physically incapable of refusing to look at photos of cats and children, so I spend the next several minutes indulging Kali by looking at photos of Valsalva scratching at a post or playing with a toy mouse.

"By the way," I say, trying to end the slide show. "You were right about Connie being evil. She jumped on me yesterday because Dr. Westin said she had to take one extra admission."

Kali beams. "Say that one more time."

"Say what?"

"The part about me being right."

I raise my eyebrows. "Uh, you were right about Connie."

Kali smiles. "First time I've heard I was right all month. I was beginning to forget what it felt like."

Amen to that.

Hours awake: 7
Chance of quitting: 18%

19

I GET AN EASY ADMISSION IN THE AFTERNOON: A young woman with a diagnosis of pyelonephritis (kidney infection). I feel like I've had a lot of pyelonephritis cases since I've been here, although I'm beginning to notice that 90% of all patients at County Hospital share one of the following ten diagnoses:

1. Chest pain, rule out heart attack
2. Heart failure
3. Cirrhosis (liver failure)
4. Emphysema/asthma
5. Kidney failure
6. Pyelonephritis
7. Stroke
8. Pneumonia
9. GI bleed
10. Alcohol/drug intoxication/overdose

I guess that's how you get to pretend to know everything: pretty much everyone has the same ten diagnoses.

This patient is named Carla Canady and she's twenty years old. Her age is good news since young patients don't stay long in the hospital and my service is gigantic. The other piece of good news is that they put her in a room with Mrs. Jefferson. That saves me at least a little bit of running around. I think I walk the equivalent of a marathon while on call.

From Ms. Canady's social history in the ER note, I discover she's the mother of a two-year-old girl. I have to say, the patients at County are making me feel like I ought to have popped out at least three kids by now. By twenty, everyone has a kid, sometimes two. And there's a tiny voice in the back of my head that wonders if I'm not doing things the wrong way. Wouldn't I be happier if I were taking care of my baby now instead of pyelonephritis patients? Isn't procreating what nature wants me to do?

Not that I have anyone to procreate with right now. Not exactly.

Ms. Canady's other problem is that she's diabetic. And she's not taking very good care of her diabetes. Actually, that's an understatement.

The test we use to measure diabetic control is called a Hemoglobin A1c. An A1c of less than 6 would mean excellent control of the diabetes. An A1c of less than 7 is good control. Ms. Canady's A1c was

13. That means she's essentially treating her diabetes with sugar pills. Literally.

I go in to talk to her, and she reminds me a lot of my teenage cousin who is always rolling her eyes and saying, "Whatever." She has on way too much make-up, especially around the eyes, especially considering she's sick and in a freaking hospital. I can't believe this girl is a mother, although she does look much older than twenty.

"You guys are giving me way too much insulin," she tells me when I come to see her.

I think if she thinks it's way too much insulin, it's probably just the right amount. "When you're sick," I say, "it's really important to keep good control of your blood sugars."

"I just have an infection though," Ms. Canady says. "Don't you treat that with, like, antibiotics?"

"Right," I say. "But if your blood sugar is controlled, your body is in better shape to fight the infection."

"But doesn't sugar turn into energy to fight infec-tions?" she says.

I almost start to launch into a big explanation, but instead I decide not to waste my breath. "No," I say. "It doesn't."

"Whatever," Ms. Canady says and rolls her eyes. But at least she doesn't protest any further. For now. I have a feeling this battle is only just beginning.

———

. . .

I END up down in the ER with Alyssa for a GI bleeder. The woman has blood coming out both ends, if you know what I mean. We were all set to admit her to our service when her blood pressure took a nosedive and she earned herself a trip to the ICU instead. Unfortunately, by the time we get done in the ER, it's after 7 p.m., meaning the cafeteria is closed.

I comment on as much while I ride upstairs in the elevator with Alyssa. As I say the words, my stomach growls pointedly.

"You should have stashed some food from lunch," Alyssa points out. I don't know where she expects me to store food since we have no fridge. In my cheeks? She whips her phone out of her pocket.

"I'm going to call my husband and ask him to bring over some fast food," she announces.

For a moment, I actually think Alyssa might offer to have her husband pick up some food for me as well, but that doesn't happen and I certainly am not going to ask. I think I'm going to have to take my chances on the food cart. I finish up a few notes and head downstairs.

Luckily, the food cart is actually there this time so I can eat something aside from popsicles. As soon as I get out, I can smell meat heating up in a big vat of oil —the stench permeates a 20-foot radius surrounding the food cart. They have a wide selection of red-checked boxes containing the various deep fried options. After quickly surveying the possibilities, I buy a box of something thickly breaded, possibly shrimp, with a side of French fries and a soda. I carry it up to the resident lounge.

If it had occurred to me that Alyssa would be in the resident lounge, I definitely wouldn't have brought my food there. I can't eat in front of Alyssa—it gives me indigestion. But instead I burst in on what is practically a party.

First of all, Connie is there, also eating a fast food burger that Alyssa clearly bought for her. And along with her is Alyssa, a pale man in his thirties with thinning black hair, and an incredibly cute toddler who is walking around the room with a French fry in each hand. The toddler has a visibly runny nose that is dripping nearly into his mouth.

"Oh," I stammer, unsure if I should stay or not. As much as I was looking forward to some time away from Alyssa, I feel like it would be rude to leave. I force a smile. "Hi."

Alyssa nods at me. She makes no motion to introduce me to her family.

I sink into one of the chairs, keeping my food on my lap. It's so deeply fried that it's hard to eat, but I force myself to take in a few bites.

The whole time, I can't stop watching Alyssa's kid. He's very cute, mostly because he looks nothing like Alyssa. He takes a bite of one fry then alternates with the other fry. And then every minute, he runs to his mom for a kiss. I wish I were one year old. Life is so simple when you're a kid. You don't even know how good you have it. Lucky bastard.

The kid's runny nose is bothering me though. He's come to Alyssa for a hug at least a dozen times and not once has she made a motion to wipe it off. Alyssa is so anal that I sometimes worry if I have one hair out of place, she'll reach over and pluck it out of my skull. How is she letting this runny nose go unchecked? Even *I* want to wipe up the snot, and trust me, I'm a huge slob.

Eventually, Alyssa's pager goes off and we all jump like a foot in the air. "You better go," she tells her husband.

He nods. "Do you think you'll be home for lunch tomorrow?"

"Probably not," Alyssa says. "My interns are still really slow."

Hey, Alyssa, said interns are sitting *right here*! And are not deaf!

Admittedly, we *are* pretty slow though.

Her husband picks up their child. He flies into a sudden panic when he realizes he's leaving. His tiny round face turns bright red, and he reaches outstretched little arms in Alyssa's direction, hollering, "Mommmmmeeeeee!!!!!"

It's sort of heartbreaking, actually. Her husband raises his eyebrows at her, but Alyssa shakes her head.

"Just go," she says. "It'll be easier."

After Alyssa's son has been dragged screaming from the room, the snot bubbling from his nostrils, she turns to us, her interns. I see whatever sadness she had is magically being converted into fury.

"Are you *still* eating?" she snaps at me.

"No," I say, quickly tossing my fried something (still not sure what the protein was) into the trash besides me.

Thankfully, my own pager goes off at that moment. And I'm almost happy to hear that Carla Canady is refusing her insulin shots because it gives me an excuse to get the hell out of there.

———

"I don't need the shots," Ms. Canady says to me. "I'm fine. Seriously."

"Your blood sugar is 326," I say.

"That's not so high," she says.

It horrifies me that she said that. A normal blood sugar is around 100. A sugar of 326 is *really* high. Maybe not high enough to send her into a diabetic coma, but pretty damn high. High enough that if she keeps walking around like that, she's going to end up being a frequent flyer at that hospital.

"I really think you should take the insulin," I tell her. "Having uncontrolled diabetes can make you really sick."

Ms. Canady just snorts and looks away from me.

"I mean, you have a daughter, right?" I say. I think of Alyssa's son being wrenched away from her. "You want to be in good health for your daughter, don't you?"

"I'll be fine," Ms. Canady says.

That's when we both hear it. The bellowing voice from the other side of the curtain, loud and pleading. It's Mrs. Jefferson.

"Please, honey, take the shots," Mrs. Jefferson says. I feel like I can nearly see her puff of white hair behind the curtain. "I have diabetes too and I used to be just like you. I never took care of it and one day I woke up half blind. You don't want to be blind. My kidneys have failed and my body has fallen apart because I didn't take care of my diabetes. I only got one leg now. My other leg—it's gone."

I see Ms. Canady staring at the curtain, her eyes wide. Mrs. Jefferson goes on: "I have a daughter too and I want to stay alive for her. I just want to see her and my grandbabies, but instead I'm stuck here in the hospital. Please, honey, take care of your body. Don't let yourself fall apart like I did. If I can convince you to do anything, please take your insulin and take care of yourself."

Ms. Canady and I are both looking at the curtain, waiting for any other words of wisdom to emerge from beyond the partition. But Mrs. Jefferson is silent.

"So," I say hopefully. "Will you take your insulin shot?"

Ms. Canady rolls her head away from the curtain. She looks me straight in the eye.

"No," she says.

I tried. Nobody could say I didn't try.

20

AT AROUND MIDNIGHT, I GET A PAGE I'VE NEVER gotten before. It's a nurse I vaguely recognize with a no-nonsense New York accent. "Dr. McGill," she says. I don't hear the scare quotes when she says "Doctor," which makes me feel good about myself, until I hear what she has to tell me: "Mr. Melendez just died."

I stare at the phone, my heart pounding. "*What*? Why didn't you call a Code Blue?"

The nurse sighs. She's like a nurse version of Alyssa. "The patient was Comfort Care. Terminal colon cancer."

"Comfort Care" means just that. The patient is no longer being treated medically, but we are keeping him comfortable until he passes away, which is expected to be imminent. Pain medications are all right, but CPR or antibiotics are not.

"So what do I do?" I ask. It seems like my work is

over if the guy's dead. I mean, that's what I'm here to prevent.

"You have to come over here and declare him dead."

"Oh."

I march over to the floor where Mr. Melendez is located. I somehow expected things to be a little more somber because a man just died, but it pretty much looks like business as usual. Two of the nurses are having a loud conversation about laxatives.

The nurse who called me, Kaitlin, is waiting for me at the nurse's station. I've worked with Kaitlin a few times before, and have always been incredibly intimidated by her. She's got at least two decades on me in age and experience, and it shows on her thin, lined face. She always wears her gray-laced black hair in a tight bun that reminds me vaguely of Julia, and today she's wearing solid purple scrubs.

"Dr. McGill?" she asks. None of the nurses know us by our names yet—we probably all seem identical to them.

I nod.

Kaitlin crooks her finger at me and leads me to Mr. Melendez's room, which is the last one in the hallway. The lights are dimmed inside and it's very quiet, at least for a hospital room. There isn't one machine beeping or alarming. I've never met Mr. Melendez before, but he looks like he was pretty sick (obviously). He's got huge hollows in his cheeks, gray stubble across his chin, and his toothless mouth is parted in a silent O. Just before a really sick patient dies, their mouth often opens that way. It's called the "O sign."

Kaitlin folds her arms across her chest and waits for me to proceed. I stand there for a minute, biting my lip.

Finally, I break down and ask, "Um, what do I do?"

Kaitlin raises her eyebrows. "You've never done this before?"

I shake my head.

She sighs. "Okay, feel for his pulse. But you won't feel anything."

I press my fingers into the grove of his wasted wrist where the radial artery runs. At first I almost think I feel a pulse, but then I realize it's my own pulse. "Okay…"

"Now you listen to his chest and make sure you don't hear anything. You won't."

I place my stethoscope on Mr. Melendez's still chest. Silence.

"And now you check his pupils."

I reach out and lift his eyelids up with my fingertips and shine a light in his pupils, which are slightly obscured by his cataracts. They don't budge.

Yep, this guy's dead all right.

The next part of the process involves paperwork, which is now my area of expertise. Essentially, I am discharging this patient. But instead of discharging him to "home" or "nursing facility," I check off the box to discharge him to "expired." Even I can't screw this one up.

As I'm flipping through the sign-out given to me on Mr. Melendez by the intern taking care of him, I notice that under "code status," he has written: "Full Code." Full Code means that in the case of Mr. Melendez going into cardiac arrest, a Code Blue should have been called.

We were supposed to try to save him.

And then I have a heart attack.

"Kaitlin!" I scream.

She drops what she's doing and rushes over to where I'm sitting. "What's wrong?"

I point out where the intern had written Mr. Melendez's code status. My heart is pounding. If we were supposed to try to save this guy, then… well, it's not *my* fault. They told me he was Comfort Care! Why oh why didn't I check the sign-out before I let him just *die*? Wait until Alyssa finds out about this…

"Oh," Kaitlin says, looking unconcerned. "Mr. Melendez's definitely Comfort Care. That intern is the biggest idiot in the hospital."

Then she flips through the chart and shows me where the patient signed the Do Not Resuscitate paperwork. I'm relieved, mostly that I didn't accidentally kill someone tonight. And that apparently the biggest idiot in the hospital isn't me. (Alyssa may beg to differ.)

As I flip through Mr. Melendez's chart, I think about the fact that a man just died. I mean, he *died*.

His life just ended right in front of me. And weirdly enough, I don't feel that sad about it. If I'm being entirely honest, I don't feel sad at all. I rented *The Joy Luck Club* last month and I cried way more in five minutes of that movie than I did over the death of a real human being. That's pretty messed up.

I should definitely feel sadder over this.

I mean, *someone* should feel sad. Like I said, a guy just died. He had no family with him, nobody shedding a tear. Someone at least should cry a little bit. *I* should cry a little bit. If I cried over *The Joy Luck Club*, I definitely should be able to cry right now. I really should.

Come on, Jane! Cry!

I sit there for a minute, waiting for tears to come. Even just a single tear. But I can't cry. I'm really just not very sad over this.

Screw it.

I flip to the front of the chart, where Mr. Melendez's emergency contacts are listed. He has one: his daughter, Carol. I dial the single number provided.

The phone rings several times, but nobody picks up. I'm about to give up when the perky voicemail recording clicks on: "Hi, this is Carol! Leave a message."

"Oh, hi," I say, a little thrown by the message. "Um, this is Dr. McGill at County Hospital. I just wanted to let you know that… your dad passed on. So, um, if you have any questions, you can just give us a call. Thanks."

As I hang up the phone, it occurs to me that I just left a *voicemail* that this woman's dad died. What the hell is *wrong* with me?

"Did you just leave a *voicemail* that someone's dad died?"

I look up and see Sexy Surgeon perched at the nurse's station, staring at me with an amused look on his face. My cheeks grow hot. "I didn't mean to…"

He laughs. "Wow, that's pretty classy. I thought you medicine interns were supposed to be all sensitive and shit?"

I glare at him. "What are you doing here, Ryan?"

"Looking for you," he says with a wink. I notice he's got a little indentation on his forehead where his surgical cap cut into his skin, and his hair is adorably tousled. I wonder how long he's been in surgery today. "Found you just in the nick of time, I think. It's clear you're in need of a break."

"I don't have time for a break," I protest.

"Fifteen minutes," Ryan says, putting his hand on my arm. And the second he touches me, I lose all ability to think rationally. I shall follow Sexy Surgeon to the ends of the Earth, if he so desires.

Fortunately, he only seems to want to go as far as the elevators. On the way to the elevators, we pass a skinny kid with disheveled brown hair and deep circles under his eyes. He looks young—even younger than me. Something about him screams out "medical student," especially the way he seems vaguely frightened of Sexy Surgeon.

"Dr. Reilly," the student says, his eyes widening. "I've been looking for you."

"You found me, Ed," Ryan says, rolling his eyes in my direction. "What's going on? How was the emergency cholecystectomy?"

"Long," Ed replies, rubbing his eyes. "Listen, I'm not on call, so… is it okay if I head home? It's after midnight."

Ryan looks him up and down, his eyes narrowing. "Didn't you get the text page I sent you about the infected graft that's coming up to the OR?"

"Yeah, but…" Ed looks at me, as if I might help him out. Fat chance, kid… I got my own troubles. "I'm not on call, so…"

"You're not on call," Ryan repeats, running the words over his tongue. "So… I guess that means you have no interest in *learning*?"

Ed's mouth falls open. "I… I'm supposed to be here at 5 a.m. tomorrow to pre-round. I just…"

"It's up to you," Ryan says with a shrug. "Obviously, I think you should go to the surgery and learn something. But if you'd rather go home and go to sleep…" He says the words *go to sleep* rather contemptuously. Sometimes I wonder if Ryan ever actually does go to sleep. "It's your decision, Ed."

Ed just stares at him for a minute. I can tell he really wants to tell Ryan to go to hell, but he doesn't dare say it. Finally, he mumbles, "I'll go to the surgery."

"Good boy," Ryan says, a slow grin spreading across his face.

I wait until Ed is gone and we're inside the elevator before I say to Ryan, "You're a complete asshole. You know that?"

Ryan laughs. "Why?"

"You could have let that med student go home."

"Well, that's no fun."

I glare at him. "Like I said, you're an asshole."

"At least *I* didn't leave a voicemail to tell someone her dad died."

He's got a point. Asshole.

When we head up in the elevator, I expect that Ryan is leading me to the call rooms and that our 15 minutes will be spent making out (nothing wrong with that). But instead, he takes me up a flight past the call rooms, to a door that appears to open to the outdoors. When he pushes it open, I realize that he's taken me to the roof of the hospital.

It doesn't look like we're supposed to be up here. It's mostly pipes and vents, although there's a single garbage bin that seems to be filled mostly with cigarettes.

The July night air is pleasantly cool up here and I feel a breeze lift the hairs that have escaped my pony-tail. Ryan takes my hand in his as he leads me to the edge of the building, and I can't help but enjoy this sweet gesture. Holding hands with him makes me feel like we're in a relationship or something, and he's not just some guy that I make out with when either of us has a free minute.

"You're not afraid of heights, are you?" he asks me.

I shake my head as I look down over the edge of the building at the tiny cars and people milling about below us, oblivious to the fact that we're looking down on them. It's a little dizzying, but there's also something really peaceful about it. Being above it all, you know?

"Don't jump," he says.

I stick out my tongue at him.

He grins. "What? You're an intern. I think it's worth saying."

The sad part is that he's probably right.

"Do you come here a lot?" I ask him.

"Yeah," he says. "I like to spit on the people walking by."

"Very funny."

His blue eyes widen. "It's true. They usually think it's rain."

"You don't really."

"Watch me."

I hear Ryan starting to hock up some spit, and I smack him in the arm. He smiles winningly at me then leans forward to kiss me.

And then we're kissing on the rooftop of a hospital. His body feels warm and firm against mine, and I can feel his hands sliding under my scrub top, touching my bare skin. He starts kissing me more hungrily, pushing me up against what I think is a drainpipe. This is so very hot. I don't want this to ever stop.

And then, of course, our pagers go off. Simultaneously.

I check the number on mine then fumble for my phone. The reception on the roof isn't very good. I notice that Ryan isn't bothering to even attempt to answer his page.

"Don't you need to call them back?" I ask him.

He winks at me. "Nah."

I sigh as I hold my phone up in the air, trying to see if I can get more than one bar of reception.

"I probably should go," I say. "I'm covering about a million patients, plus I've got the biggest service in the hospital already."

"Is that so?" Ryan asks.

"It's so," I confirm. "So don't even think about trying to dump Mrs. Coughlin back on me."

"I'd say there's zero percent chance of that happening."

"Really? How come?"

"Because she's dead."

I lower my phone and stare at Ryan. He isn't smiling or doing anything else to indicate that he's joking. "Are you serious?"

"Yeah." He shrugs. "She died on the operating table."

"Oh my God…" I cover my mouth with my hand. "That's… horrible."

"I guess so," Ryan says. "I mean, it's not like she was young and healthy. Even if the operation was a success, she still wasn't going to last long with metastatic pancreatic cancer."

He leans against the edge of the building, the wind tousling his hair. I don't see the slightest trace of sadness or remorse on his face.

"How could you not care that she died?" I ask him.

He snorts. "Are you seriously giving me shit over this? Were you sad over that guy you just pronounced dead?"

"A little," I lie.

Ryan rolls his eyes.

"Anyway, that's different," I insist. "I didn't know that guy at all. You knew Mrs. Coughlin."

"Barely."

"She liked you," I say.

"So?" He grins. "Everyone likes me."

I fold my arms across my chest. "*I* don't like you."

He tugs on the drawstring of my scrubs and I wait just a beat too long before I swat him away.

"Yeah, you're just hot for me," he says.

My pager goes off again and I realize that if I don't answer it soon, there's going to be a SWAT team up here searching for me. Anyway, I can tell that getting Sexy Surgeon to feel any real emotion over a patient is a lost cause.

Although the scary truth is, I'm not entirely sure how sad I am either. As I head back downstairs, I seem to be unable to squeeze out even one tear on her behalf. But at least I try.

Hours awake: 20
Chance of Sexy Surgeon ever growing the hell up: 1%

21

"How much Lasix is Mr. Sanchez getting?" Dr. Westin asks me.

It's the twenty-eighth hour. I'm sitting at the nurse's station with Alyssa and Dr. Westin, near Mr. Sanchez's room. Mr. Sanchez, the pregnant man, has now reduced his gestation to about four or five months. We're going to send him home. I'm all set to send him home, and have been surreptitiously writing his discharge summary during every free moment. I've gotten to be really good at writing while walking up and down stairs.

"Uh," I say. I start shuffling through the stack of papers I'm holding.

"Jane," Alyssa says, "you have to be ready to answer when the attending asks you a question."

Good advice. Except it doesn't make me find Mr. Sanchez's med list any faster.

"I'll go check the nurse's med book," Dr. Westin says, leaping to his feet.

Alyssa watches Dr. Westin run off. As soon as he's out of sight, she leans in so close to me that I can feel her hot breath on my neck: "The attending does not stand."

I stare at her. "What?"

"If the attending asks you a question," Alyssa says, "you get up and find out the answer. You do *not* let the attending stand. *Ever.*"

Hey, maybe I should just carry the attending on my shoulders during rounds. Would that be okay, *Alyssa*? And if you're so gung-ho on never letting the attending stand, why didn't *you* go look up the medications?

I've composed about ten angry replies to Alyssa in my head, none of which I have the courage to say, when Dr. Westin returns. "He's on 40 mg twice a day!"

And of course, at that moment, I discover the paper with Mr. Sanchez's meds on it. But it's probably good I didn't find it earlier, since I had the dose wrong.

"Jane," Alyssa says in an inquiring tone, and I wince inwardly. No more questions, please! I am way too tired for this. "How long did you spend yesterday waiting on the phone for the translator for Mr. Sanchez?"

I don't really understand the point of Alyssa's question. I've been awake for a long time, and it's not clear why it matters how much of my life I wasted on hold for the translator. It's over. Why waste more time on it?

"I don't know," I finally say. "Ten minutes?"

"Mr. Sanchez *speaks English*," Alyssa says triumphantly.

I don't know what she expects me to make of this revelation. All I can say is, "He does?"

Dr. Westin chuckles, "Gina, you didn't know your patient speaks English?"

"Did you even *try* to talk to him?" Alyssa asks me, shaking her head at disgust at my lack of effort.

I tried. He doesn't freaking speak English! "I did."

"We had a great talk this morning," Alyssa says pointedly. "I was telling him about the diet he needs to keep due to his cirrhosis and he asked me all sorts of really intelligent questions. Jane, you really have to make more of an effort to communicate with your patients."

I swear, Mr. Sanchez did not speak English when I met him yesterday. The only solution I can think of is that the man somehow learned to speak it within the last 24 hours. It's a miracle.

The three of us march into Mr. Sanchez's room together. He's showered this morning, his face is scrubbed clean, and his black hair is brushed and slicked back. It's amazing how so many of my patients look like they just spent a night at a fancy resort.

"Hello, Mr. Sanchez," Alyssa says cheerfully.

"Hello," he replies. I swear, if he starts speaking fluent English, I'll cry.

"Mr. Sanchez," she says. "I was just telling the team about our talk this morning. About all the foods you said you're going to avoid."

He nods and a pleasant smile appears on his face. "Ah. Yes."

She folds her arms across her chest, getting ready to show off. "Tell the team what you're going to avoid eating."

I hold my breath. Mr. Sanchez looks between the three of us. Finally, he says, "*Qué?*"

Alyssa's eyes widen. "Mr. Sanchez, don't you remember? You're not going to eat…?"

He keeps the pleasant smile plastered on his lips. "*Qué?*"

"Salt!" Alyssa blurts out. "Salt. You're not going to eat salt, right?"

"*Sal?*" Mr. Sanchez raises his eyebrows. I look over at Dr. Westin, who is trying not to laugh. Alyssa's face is a shade of bright pink.

I love you, Mr. Sanchez. Just for that, I'm giving you a few tablets of Percocet to go.

Hours awake: 29
Chance of quitting: 19%

22

LIKE I SAID, I'M NOT A HUGE FAN OF NAPS.

But when you hardly slept on call, they are a necessary evil. It does feel sort of nice to fall into my bed after being awake for I-don't-want-to-think-about-how-many-hours. Sometimes I think I fall asleep before my head even hits the pillow.

But no matter what, waking up is always a disorienting experience. I am never entirely sure where I am and why I'm first waking up in the mid-evening. Especially when what wakes me up is a pounding at my door. That will not stop no matter how hard I stare at the door and silently plead for it to stop.

Finally, I stumble out of bed and throw open the door. Unsurprisingly, it's Julia. Also unsurprisingly, she doesn't look the least bit tired, despite likely being as sleep-deprived as I am. And her ponytail is absolutely perfect as usual.

"Jane," she says, her unidentifiable accent nearly a monotone. "You got my note? About the bathroom?"

"Oh," I say. "Yeah."

Is today one of my days to clean? If it is, then that's too damn bad. There is no way in hell I'm cleaning any bathrooms right now.

"Did you see the receipt?" Julia says, raising her eyebrows.

I groan inwardly. Right, I have to pay Julia for the stupid cleaning supplies.

"Hang on," I say.

After a brief search, I locate my purse, which is under a pile of scrubs. I pull out my wallet, and retrieve two twenty-dollar bills and four ones. I'm now left with only a five-dollar bill to my name. I think I'm going to be mostly eating ramen noodles for a while.

I bring the twenties and the ones over to Julia and hand them over with a twinge of regret. She counts the money then frowns at me.

"What?" I say.

Julia holds up the bills. "It was 44 dollars and *67 cents*."

You have *got* to be kidding me.

I take the four one-dollar bills back from her and hand over my five. Oh well. Ones are better for the vending machines anyway.

When I give Julia the money, she says, "I'll get you change." I almost tell her to forget it, but then I remember that I can use the change for the vending machines too. I'm not nearly rich enough to turn down 33 cents.

Days living with my crazy roommate: A million billion
Chances I will be doing a half-assed cleaning the bathroom in the very near future: 110%

23

CALL #4

My latest admission claims she hasn't been poisoned but I have good reason to be skeptical.

This is 62-year-old Gloria Vargas's second admission for chest pain. She's a tiny, dark-skinned woman who has been rubbing the left side of her chest every few minutes as I talk to her. I have her old chart from her first admission, which I obtained after Alyssa screamed at me for five straight minutes about how it wasn't possible to see a patient if you didn't review their old chart first. On her first chest pain admission, Mrs. Vargas's urine tested positive for amphetamines. It came out that her husband had slipped some meth into her morning coffee. Because caffeine sometimes just isn't enough to get you going.

The first thing I did was order a urine tox on her to check for amphetamines again. One thing I'm learning from working at County Hospital is that nobody ever admits to taking drugs. Even when confronted with the results of a positive urine tox, they will stare you right in the eyes and swear on their life they never snorted cocaine. If that's true, then how did it get in your pee, huh? A visit from the cocaine fairies?

"I didn't take any meth this time," Mrs. Vargas swears to me from her hospital bed, looking me straight in the eye.

Yeah, right.

"My husband had a drug problem," she says to me, her brown eyes wide and earnest. "But he's gotten help."

Sure he has.

"He's better now."

Sure he is.

"Also," she says with a mischievous smile. "I make my own coffee now. Just in case."

"You know we got a urine tox screen," I remind her.

"Rightfully so," she says. She laughs. "I wouldn't trust me either."

She rubs her chest then. Her hands are very steady, in spite of everything. I bite my lip. I don't want to be that naïve intern who keeps getting taken in by the drug addicts. I really don't.

"I used to be a nurse, you know," Mrs. Vargas says.

"You did?" I say, looking at her with a newfound respect. And nervousness. Whenever I take care of a healthcare provider, I always worry they'll figure out I don't know what I'm doing. They'll realize that when I'm putting my stethoscope on their chest every single morning, I'm not really listening half the time.

She nods. "Before my back went out. I worked in pediatrics." She gets a misty look in her eyes. "I miss it."

Crap. She's actually starting to make me believe she didn't take meth.

I mean, it's *possible*. She doesn't look like she's high. She's not shaking or saying bizarre things. And she seems like such a nice lady. I really want to believe her urine tox is going to be negative.

I mean, just because I'm working at County Hospital, does that necessarily mean everyone has to be a drug addict?

Don't answer that.

———

I SNEAK up to the call room to have my lunch because I feel like I need a few minutes of quiet. The call rooms are incredibly quiet during the day. Nobody goes to that floor in the daytime aside from the cleaning staff. I feel like it's more peaceful than my apartment, because there's no risk of Julia pounding on the door and accusing me of, like, stealing a grain of rice or something.

I settle down at the desk with my sandwich of

chicken with pesto sauce, which sounds good yet still manages to be sort of ruined by the cafeteria. The pesto is runny and the chicken is dry, but it's edible. I swallow my first bite when I hear a knock at the door to the call room. It's probably housekeeping, come to change the sheets.

"Come back later!" I yell at the door. "Room occupied! *Ocupado*!"

"No, must change sheets now!" an accented male voice yells back.

Bastard. I put down my sandwich and sprint to the door, and yank it open to give the housekeeper a piece of my mind. Except it isn't housekeeping.

"Ryan!" As I swat at him, I can't help but notice the firmness of his chest. Why does he have to keep being so damn sexy? "You're an asshole."

He grins at me. "Are you saying you don't want me to change your sheets?"

"I'm eating lunch, you know," I say, pointing at my sandwich.

"Lunch is for the weak," Ryan says. I have to admit, I'm not certain if I've ever seen him sit down for an actual meal.

"Well, then I'm weak."

My pager goes off at that moment and I'm 99% sure it's Alyssa, wanting to hear about Mrs. Vargas and her chest pain. My few minutes of peace are over.

"Go ahead," Ryan says. "Return the page. I'll entertain myself."

The room is equipped with a phone, so I sit down

on the bed and call Alyssa back. I tell her about Mrs. Vargas, and explain about the prior history of the positive urine tox, but that I actually think she's telling the truth this time. She really didn't seem like she was on meth.

As I'm talking on the phone, Ryan sits at the other end of the bed, takes my left leg in his hand and removes my Dansko clog. He places my foot on his lap and starts massaging my toes, my forefoot, then my heel and ankle. As I read off Mrs. Vargas's cardiac enzymes to Alyssa, I feel Ryan's fingers slipping up my scrub pants and massaging my calf. Crap, when was the last time I shaved my legs? Oh, who cares?

"Jane?" Alyssa's voice on the phone seems very far away.

"Huh?" I say.

She sighs. "Are you still awake?"

"Yes, I'm sorry," I mumble. Ryan snorts loudly and I give him a look. "Can you repeat that?"

"I said I'll meet you in the resident lounge in ten minutes," Alyssa says. "We need to do your mid-rotation feedback."

Oh, joy.

I put down the phone and glare at Ryan, who has an amused look on his face. "Did you get taken in by another drug addict?" he asks me.

"No," I huff. "She's telling the truth. I'm pretty sure."

"Come on, Jane…"

"Not everyone is a liar," I say, as I pick up my

sandwich and take an extra-large bite. If Alyssa says we're meeting in ten minutes, she really means five.

"I bet you anything that urine tox is positive," Ryan retorts.

I fold my arms across my chest. "You're on. It's a bet." Mrs. Vargas, don't let me down! "What are the terms?"

He thinks for a minute. "If I win, then… I get to second base."

I raise my eyebrows. "And second base is…?"

"Full access to boobies."

I laugh. "Seriously? Okay, and what if I win?"

Ryan's hand moves up my calf and rests on my bare knee. "Then *you* get to second base."

"And what's second base for me?"

He waggles his eyebrows at me.

"You've *got* to be kidding me." I roll my eyes.

"Fine. What do you want then?"

I think for a minute. "If I win, then you take me out tomorrow night for dinner. And not to the cafeteria and not to a bar. It's got to be an actual restaurant with waiters and real seats."

"Real seats?" Ryan makes a face. "Damn, I didn't know you were so high maintenance."

"And you can't wear scrubs," I say. Because I desperately want to know what Ryan looks like in real clothes.

"I'm not sure I own anything other than scrubs," he says.

"Take it or leave it."

"Okay, deal."

Ryan holds out his hand to me and we shake on it. I can't help but feel that either way, I'm going to come out a winner on this.

Hours awake: 9
Chance of Mrs. Vargas having a positive urine tox: Who am I kidding? Like, 99%.

24

I GET DOWN TO THE RESIDENT LOUNGE SIX MINUTES later, part of the chicken pesto sandwich still lodged in my throat. Naturally, Alyssa is already waiting for me, and looks at her watch pointedly when I arrive. She seems furious. I play a little game where I try to guess what made her so angry before she has a chance to tell me.

"Did you even *examine* Mrs. Vargas?" she asks me.

I just stare at her for a minute until I realize this wasn't a rhetorical question.

"Um, yeah. I did."

"Her pupils are *huge*," Alyssa practically spits at me. "She's high as a kite! How could you not notice that?"

Her pupils are huge? Wow, I completely missed that finding. Her pupils looked completely normal to me. Well, I guess Sexy Surgeon is getting to second base.

"Oh," is all I say.

Alyssa nods as if she expected nothing less of me at this point. I sit down on the couch across from her and fold my hands together. My knees are shaking a little so I try to steady them with my folded hands.

"So let's do some feedback," Alyssa says.

"Okay," I say. I tug on my scrub top, which suddenly feels much too hot.

Alyssa tucks her index cards away in her white coat pocket and stares at me intently. It's a little unnerving. "So how do you think you've been doing?"

"I'll be honest," I say. "It's been a rough transition. I did mostly electives and traveled during my fourth year of med school, so I lost some of the knowledge I had since my sub-internship. But I feel like I'm getting back up to speed."

Alyssa nods. "Yes, I'd agree with that." Then she starts in with, "No offense, but…"

Immediately, I brace myself. Whenever someone starts a sentence with "no offense but," it means they're going to say something really offensive. I hate that phrase. No offense, but if you say that, you're a jackass.

In any case, pretty much everything Alyssa has ever said to me has been offensive. So if she thinks it's particularly offensive, then I am definitely worried.

"No offense," Alyssa says, "but your knowledge and skill level is more like… well, like a medical student."

Hey, Alyssa, newsflash: I was a medical student *two weeks ago*. Sheesh.

"You need to be constantly reading," she says. "Every night. You need to read vehemently."

Read *vehemently*? What the hell does that mean? How do you read vehemently? "Okay," I say.

"Because your knowledge level is really pretty poor," she says.

"Uh huh."

"Compared with your peers like Connie, you're really not up to par," she says.

I glare at her. Here's the thing: My medical board scores? You know, the ones that objectively test your knowledge of the field of medicine? Pretty high. Maybe not as high as Sexy Surgeon or Connie's scores, but I have a feeling that I could give Alyssa a run for her money. So my knowledge level isn't bad. It's probably over one standard deviation above average, if the medical licensing board is to be trusted. But there's a huge difference between having knowledge and feeling comfortable using that knowledge on actual human beings who could *die* if you do the wrong thing.

But all I say is, "Okay."

I sit there, waiting for Alyssa to ask me for feedback on herself. It seems like she'd want to know how she's performing as a senior resident, and in my experience, that's always been part of the feedback process. But she doesn't ask me and I don't offer.

I guess she's comfortable in the knowledge that she's perfect.

My pager goes off and Alyssa nods consent that I may answer. I feel like I only vaguely remember what it was like to be able to do things like eat, pee, and make a call without first asking permission. "This is Dr. McGill," I say.

"Hello, Doctor," a nurse says. "I have a question on Mr. Stevens in Room 428B. He says he keeps a gun by his bed at home and he wants it now."

"Yeah, that's not going to happen," I say.

"He says he doesn't want to use it," the nurse explains. "He just wants to keep it by his bed."

"The answer is still no," I say. Are they seriously calling me about this?

"Wait," the nurse says. "Another nurse wants to talk to you."

I hang on the phone while Alyssa checks her watch. Finally, a second nurse comes on the line. "Doctor," she says. "Thomas Jefferson is here and really wants to talk to you." And then she dissolves into giggles. Appropriately so.

I sigh and look up at Alyssa. "I have to go," I say to her.

She nods. Thomas Jefferson is a true American hero. First he helped found the country and now he's getting me out of a conversation with Alyssa.

———

· · ·

I CAN HARDLY BELIEVE it when I lay my eyes on
Thomas Jefferson. I expected him to be big and bois-
terous like his wife Marquette, but instead, he's a tiny
fellow. He's only maybe an inch or two taller than me
and skinny as a rail. His black hair is cropped very
close to his skull, but he makes up for it with a graying
beard that goes down to his shirt collar.

"I am so sorry, Dr. Jane," Mrs. Jefferson says when
I walk into the room. "I told him not to bother you
when you're working."

"That's all right," I say. "I was happy to come
here."

Mrs. Jefferson beams at her husband. "What did I
tell you? Isn't she a sweetheart?"

"Marquette tells me she's in capable hands,"
Thomas Jefferson says in a deep, crackly voice. He
reaches into a bag he's holding and pulls out what
looks like a cake box. "I brought you this."

I take the box from him and peer inside. It's a
mishmash of different fruits placed haphazardly in a
grayish custard, enveloped by a slightly blackened
crust. It looks like it was made by a couple of overly
zealous kindergarteners. "What is it?"

"Fruit custard pie," Thomas Jefferson says
proudly. "It's my sister's specialty. She made it up just
for you."

I look up at Mrs. Jefferson, who is shaking her
head. "Alma and those pies…"

Not wanting to get involved in a family argument, I clutch the pie to my chest and say, "Thank you very much."

"See?" Thomas Jefferson says. "She likes it!"

"She's just being nice!" Mrs. Jefferson retorts.

"That pie won a contest once!" Thomas Jefferson argues.

"What contest was that?" Mrs. Jefferson shoots back. "Pie most likely to give you the runs?"

"I better go," I say abruptly.

I scurry out of the room, holding the pie (which there is no way in hell I am eating). It takes me several seconds after I've left the room to realize that Thomas Jefferson has followed me outside. He's got a worried look on his small face.

"Dr. Jane," he says. "Can I talk to you?"

I put the cake down at the nurse's station and nod at him. "Sure. What's up?"

He heaves a sigh. I can see tears forming in his brown eyes. "It's all my fault that this happened to Markie."

I stare at him. "What?"

He wipes his left eye with the back of his hand. "When she had that infection," he says, "she didn't want to get the amputation. She didn't want to lose her leg. But I talked her into it. I told her she'd get home faster if she did what the doctors said. I didn't know they'd end up taking the whole leg…" A tear rolls down his cheek. "And now it looks like she ain't never coming home, Dr. Jane."

"That's…" I hesitate, the words catching in my throat. "That's not necessarily true."

"I can't take care of her, Dr. Jane," he says. "I'm not a young man and I got heart problems of my own. She wants *so bad* just to come home and see her grandkids."

We want it bad too. Living in the hospital is not the most cost-efficient thing Mrs. Jefferson could be doing. She should be going home. We've got social workers trying to navigate the system, trying to find a way to make it happen. But I don't have much hope right now. We can't even send her to a nursing home because her insurance won't pay for it, so none of them will accept her.

"We're doing our best," is what I say to Thomas Jefferson.

He nods and pats my shoulder. "I know you are," he says. "I just had to say my piece."

Then he turns and I watch his narrow shoulders as he disappears back into his wife's hospital room.

———

THERE'S a quiet room on the fourth floor of the hospital that contains four computers and three phones, where residents often go to check labs. The computers are very slightly faster than the one in the lounge, although still significantly slower than anything that could be purchased on the market today. I'm at one of the computers, waiting for it to log me in, and Kali is next to me talking on the phone. I can't help but listen in to her conversation.

"No, I discharged him!" Kali is yelling into the phone, her tiny elfin face red. "He has to go home. Now." She rolls her eyes at me. "I don't *care* if he doesn't have shoes! Not having shoes is *not* a reason to be hospitalized."

I cover my mouth to suppress a laugh. Kali scribbles something on a sheet of paper then passes it in my direction.

It says: "Code Dinner!" I nod.

"So why won't he wear the shoes you offered him?" Kali says into the phone. I hear her groan loudly. "They smell like chemicals and he thinks they're unsafe? Seriously? Isn't this the guy who overdosed on heroin? Tell him the shoes are safer than heroin."

I turn my attention back to my computer, which has finally logged me on. Mrs. Vargas's labs are back from earlier, including her urine tox. Considering Alyssa's observation about her pupil size, I'm expecting to see a positive result for amphetamines. But instead the urine tox is completely negative. I was right—Mrs. Vargas is drug-free.

Holy crap, I was right!

And now Ryan Reilly has to take me out to dinner. Which is great, but really, I'm mostly looking forward to telling Alyssa I was right. That, let me tell you, will be sweet.

Kali gets off the phone and I can see she's trying to compose herself. "I need food," she says. "Stat."

I nod. "Let's hit the cafeteria."

Maybe I'll see Alyssa there and get to rub it in her face that she was wrong wrong wrong.

Kali and I pass the resident lounge on the way to the cafeteria. The door is slightly ajar and I suddenly hear Alyssa's voice coming from inside.

I tap Kali on the shoulder, "You go ahead. I'll catch up with you."

"No, please come, Jane," she whines. "I don't want to get stuck sitting with Julia."

"Two minutes," I say. "I promise."

Kali has no choice but to acquiesce. I push my hand against the door to the lounge and Alyssa's voice gets louder. I realize that she's talking on the phone. I enter the room, but she's turned toward the window and doesn't notice me.

"Can you say 'bye bye' to mama?" Alyssa is saying into the phone in that high, sweet voice. It's her son, I guess. "Please, sweetie, just say something to mama." She pauses. "Please, say something. Say *anything*…"

There's a long pause and I shift where I'm standing. I left the Jeffersons' pie in here earlier for residents to graze on. Despite how disgusting it looked to me and the real possibility of it being a source of gastroenteritis, there's now only one sliver of pie remaining in the box. I wonder if Alyssa ate any pie.

I turn my attention back to Alyssa, who is now quiet. Finally she speaks again in a normal voice. "I know, he's shy on the phone," she says. "I know. Just tell him I'll be home tomorrow. Maybe I'll make it for lunch."

When she puts down the phone, her narrow lips are set in a straight line. The smart thing for me to do would have been to get the hell out, but I seem to be frozen in place. She whirls around and catches me standing there. "Jane!" she snaps at me. "What are you doing here?"

Wishing I were anywhere else. "Mrs. Vargas's urine tox came back," I say lamely. "It was negative."

She nods, as if this is the least interesting piece of news she'd heard all day. She doesn't apologize to me for saying I was wrong, that's for sure.

"By the way, Jane," she says. "I've been meaning to talk to you about your white coat."

I finger the stiff material of the coat covering my scrubs. It's a bit big and the sleeves come down nearly to the tip of my thumbs. "What about it?"

"Look at it!" Alyssa snaps at me.

I look at the coat. "Um…"

"Look how wrinkled it is!" she says. "I would say it's at an unacceptable level of wrinkles. Is this the level of professionalism you want to show?"

Is she kidding me? Am I supposed to be spending my time *ironing* my white coat? Seriously, it's not *that* wrinkled.

"And what's this?" Alyssa says, pointing at a faded

yellow spot on my left sleeve, about a centimeter in diameter.

"I guess it's a stain," I admit.

Alyssa just shakes her head, as if she is too horribly disappointed for words. But what am I supposed to do? The hospital only provided me with two white coats. I can't launder them on a daily basis. Not when I'm also cleaning the bathroom every other day.

I just have to face the fact that no matter what I do, I can never live up to Alyssa's standards.

Hours awake: 13
Chance of quitting: 65%

25

EVEN IN MY DREAMS, I AM WORKING. YOU'D THINK I could take six or seven hours off from my job, but apparently I can't.

In my dream, I'm in the hospital, working up a new admission while Alyssa watches me. The patient has pain and I ask where the pain is. *Everywhere,* the patient tells me. I ask him to be more specific. *Everywhere in my body,* he clarifies. I try to write down his comment but I can't find my notes. Or a pen.

You have to be more prepared, Jane, Alyssa snaps at me. I apologize and start searching for a pen in my pockets, but just keep pulling out packets and packets of gauze while Alyssa continues to scream at me.

Unbelievable. Even in my dreams, I can't stand up to Alyssa and tell her what I really think of her.

I wake up from my post-call nap feeling completely disoriented as usual. I probably would have slept well into the evening, but I get woken up by my cell phone ringing. I grab for it, and mumble, "'Lo?"

A familiar voice says into the phone: "I can pick you up in one hour. Just name the restaurant."

It's Sexy Surgeon. I texted him my triumph in the urine tox, and he's ready to make good on his end of the bet: buying me dinner. Except I am so damn tired. "Oh," I say.

"I found at least five restaurants in New York that all have chairs and waiters," he says. "We can go wherever you want. Sky's the limit, babe."

I groan. "I'm so tired. I just want pizza."

"Jane, you are my kind of woman."

An hour later, Ryan and I are heading out to the nearest pizza joint. Even though this isn't exact how I pictured our romantic evening together, I have to admit, he made the effort. For one thing, he's not wearing scrubs. He's wearing a navy blue T-shirt and faded blue jeans, and I can tell he's showered and shaved recently. I can smell his aftershave and it's making me a little giddy.

Luckily, the closest pizza parlor is actually very good. I must be hungry because I can smell the oil and cheese halfway down the block, and my stomach rumbles. As we walk in, they're pulling a fresh pie out of the oven and the cheese is all hot and bubbly. I order two slices of cheese pizza at the counter and Ryan gets three. There are all sorts of crazy toppings on the pizzas, like one slice has ziti on it, but I feel like a really good pizza doesn't need anything but the pizza.

"You're a pizza snob, I bet," Ryan says to me as we settle into our seats. He slides his three paper plates of pizza onto the red-and-white-checked tablecloth.

"What does that mean?" (I actually know what he means. I am totally a pizza snob.)

"You've got to have your pizza the classic New York-style, or else it won't do," he says. "Like you probably think Chicago deep dish is disgusting."

"Well," I say, "not *disgusting*, but… well…"

Ryan grins at me. "Pizza snob."

I huff at him and take a bite of my pizza, which is still piping hot from the oven. I can tell that I'm going to polish this off in like two minutes. I try to slow down for Ryan's sake.

"Where are you from?" he asks me. He takes a guess: "Brooklyn?"

"No, Queens."

Ryan lifts his hand in the air so I can high-five him. Which I do, mostly as an excuse to touch him.

"Why am I high-fiving you?" I ask.

He points to his chest. "I'm from Fresh Meadow."

"Jamaica," I say.

"Tell me," he says, "when you say that to most people, do they ask you how come you don't have a Caribbean accent?"

I laugh. "Yes!"

Ryan shakes his head. "People are so dumb."

I find out from Ryan that his father is a lawyer and his mother a teacher. He's got two siblings, an older brother and an older sister.

"My sister Maggie went the teacher route too," he says. "She's got two kids and lives in Long Island."

"How about your brother?" I ask.

Ryan hesitates. "Sean is… still figuring things out."

For some reason, I get the sense that Ryan is being kind of evasive when he talks about his family. I can't imagine why, because the Reillys seem pretty picture perfect compared to what I grew up with. He certainly has nothing to be ashamed of.

"By the way," Ryan says to me as he finishes off the crust of his first slice. "What can I do to make you smile a little more at work? Seriously, you walk around looking like someone just died."

I jut out my chin. "Maybe someone *did* just die."

"It's a hospital, Jane. Not a morgue."

"Well, sorry."

"Don't apologize," he says. "I just feel bad you're so unhappy."

"I *am* an intern," I point out. "Weren't you miserable as an intern?"

"No way." Ryan looks me in the eyes and I can tell he means it. "As long as I got to be in the OR, I was happy. I freakin' love operating."

"Goody for you."

"Come on," he says. "I know you're in *Medicine* and all, but you can't be unhappy *all* the time. I mean, why'd you go to med school in the first place?"

"To help people," I answer, almost automatically.

"Okay, liar," Ryan laughs. "I'm not the admissions committee, you know. You can be honest."

Can I? I study Ryan's face and decide to trust him. "My dad left my mom when I was little," I say. "She was broke my whole childhood, and… she didn't want that to happen to me."

Ryan is quiet for a minute. "If that's the reason you went to med school," he says, "no wonder you're miserable."

"Gee, thanks." I throw a crumbled up napkin at him and he ducks. "It's not entirely awful. I mean, I really do like helping people. I like knowing that the purpose of my job is to make sick people well. Most of the time it's just routine and following algorithms, but every once in a while, you get to really make a difference."

"You sound like you're in a pageant," he comments. He raises the pitch of his voice mockingly: "*My name is Jane McGill and I want to make sick people well.*"

I throw a second napkin at him and this one hits him square in the chest, leaving behind a glob of tomato sauce. "Hey!" he protests.

"You're obnoxious."

Ryan grins. "You totally had that coming. Anyway, you know you love it."

Gah! I hate that I find him so sexy when he's been

a complete jackass. And I hate it worse that he knows it.

After we finish off our pizza slices (and go back for seconds… thank God scrubs have drawstrings), Ryan insists on walking me home. When we get to my front door, he hesitates.

"Do you want to come in?" I offer. I tug playfully at the sleeve of his shirt. "I'll let you get to second base."

His eyes light up. "Yeah? I thought I lost that bet."

"We can call it a draw."

We fall into the apartment together, kissing and groping wildly at each other. Funny how I'm not tired at all anymore. And if Julia comes out and interrupts this, I swear to God I will murder her.

26

SHORT CALL

GOING INTO SHORT CALL, CONNIE HAS WON THE game.

"Winning the game" means she managed to discharge all her patients. I don't know how she does it. Maybe she has some magic tonic she feeds to everyone to get them well. Maybe if Mrs. Jefferson were her patient, she'd have grown her leg back by now.

Although I do end up getting some amazing news on arrival to the hospital. The social worker Robyn greets me on the floor and says to me, "Jane! I got visiting nursing services covered for Mrs. Jefferson!"

I can hardly believe my ears. "You didn't!"

"I did!" Robyn cries. I've worked with Robyn many times in the past month and she always seems a little jaded and dejected. But now her lined eyes are lit up. "It's all arranged!"

I stand there, savoring this information. I may actually get to discharge my rock star. Wow.

"That's wonderful," I say. "You're amazing, Robyn."

Robyn buffs her fingernails on her shirt. "Just in a day's work," she laughs. Then she adds, "The only snag is that she still needs IV antibiotics for her infection, right?"

I nod. "Three more weeks."

"Does she have a PICC line?"

A PICC line is a central line that is usually inserted for long term antibiotics, because it can stay in place longer than other kinds of lines. Mrs. Jefferson has been getting her antibiotics through an IV in her arm, but she definitely can't keep that at home.

"I'll arrange it," I promise.

County Hospital has a special nurse who inserts PICC lines. I've heard you have to sell your soul to get her to come insert one, but at this point, I'm willing to make the trade.

Mrs. Jefferson is even happier about her discharge than I am, which is probably appropriate since she's the one who's actually going home. When I walk into her room, she bursts into tears.

"I can't wait, Dr. Jane," she sniffles. "I just want to play with my grandkids again."

Each of her grandchildren has drawn her a card, and they're plastered on the walls around her room.

By the backwards writing on the card, I'd guess none of them is much older than kindergarten age.

"I'm really happy for you," I tell her.

"Thank you so much, Dr. Jane," she says. "Thank you for everything you done for me. I'll never forget it."

"You're welcome," I say, even though I didn't actually do anything. Robyn is the real hero. I've just been a glorified babysitter.

———

It might make sense to give Connie more patients on short call to even out our discrepancy, but Connie's already made it very clear how she feels about that. So the first patient of the morning goes to me.

The patient's name is Jean Rogers. She came to us from a nursing home with altered mental status, meaning she's tired and confused as hell. She was diagnosed in the ER with a urinary tract infection but she hasn't perked up yet despite a few doses of antibiotics. So it's up to us to figure out the mystery.

When I get to the hallway where Mrs. Rogers's room is located, I smell something terrible. I lift my head, sniffing just hard enough to identify the smell. I have no idea what it is.

That's when I see a nurse emerge from Mrs.

Rogers's room wearing a facemask. I raise my eyebrows at the nurse.

"Is she on droplet precautions?" I ask. Droplet precautions are used when a patient has an infection colonizing the mucous membranes of their nose or mouth, which thereby spreads into the air. It basically means everyone who enters the room has to wear a mask.

The nurse shakes her head at me. "No, it just smells really bad in there. I couldn't take it. I thought I was going to throw up."

Well, that's just great.

I brace myself as I enter the room. The stench hits me like a punch in the nose.

There are a lot of really bad smells in the hospital. If I had to rate the worst of them, I would do so accordingly:

1. Clostridium difficile colitis, which causes a really smelly diarrhea
2. Rectal gangrene
3. Vomit
4. Gastrointestinal bleed
5. Rectal abscess

But I literally have never smelled anything this awful before in my life. I look at Mrs. Rogers, a withered, wrinkled body lying in the hospital bed. There's no way she weighs more than a hundred pounds soaking wet. How is it possible such a powerful smell could come from her?

All I know is that nearly all the really bad smells come from the rectal area, so Alyssa will have my head if I don't check her down there.

Dallas, I'm going in. At least this time I've got my guaiac cards.

———

I HAVE LITERALLY CHECKED every orifice of Mrs. Rogers's body and I can't identify where that smell is coming from. And it's not going away. If anything, the smell is growing in intensity. It seems like a distinct possibility that in another 24 hours, the whole hospital will smell like Mrs. Rogers. In 48 hours, the entire city. In 72 hours, the entire world.

And only I, Jane McGill, slightly incompetent medicine intern, have the power to stop it.

The first thing I do is call the nursing home to get Mrs. Rogers's old records (I know, Medicine is so glamorous). We need to get a little more history. For all I know, she's smelled like this her whole life.

"We'll send you the records right away," the woman at the nursing home promises me.

"Thanks, I really appreciate it," I say.

I run to the bathroom to scrub my hands really well. I keep an eye out for Ryan, because I don't want to run into him right now. I feel certain the stench of Mrs. Rogers is clinging to my clothes and hair. I'm going to have to douse myself in Julia's organic bleach to get rid of it.

When I return from the bathroom, the records have not yet been faxed. I start writing up my note on Mrs. Rogers, keeping an eye on the fax machine, but still nothing. Finally, I decide to give them another call.

"Hello," I say. "This is Dr. McGill at County Hospital. I'm waiting for the records on Jean Rogers."

A bored female voice says into the phone, "Who?"

"Jean Rogers. She's a resident at your facility."

"Who did you talk to before?" the woman asks.

I stare at the phone. "I have no idea."

"When you talk to someone on the phone, you need to ask them for their name," the woman says accusingly.

"Well, how many of you are there over there?" I retort.

The woman seems none too pleased with me right now. "I'll see if we can send those records to you again."

"And what's *your* name?" I start to ask, but she's already hung up on me. Damn. How am I supposed to get peoples' names if they just hang up on me?

An hour later, I still have not received any faxes from the nursing home. And the nurses are spraying air freshener all over the hallway where Mrs. Rogers's room is located. This is getting serious.

I call the nursing home again and this time I get another unfamiliar voice answering. I wish I had the names of any of the people I'd spoken to so far.

"This is Dr. McGill," I say in a voice that, I have to admit, is not loaded with patience. "This is the third time I'm calling to get the medical records faxed over on Jean Rogers."

What the woman on the other line says to me manages to completely shock me: "Oh, we don't have a fax machine."

I stare at the phone. "What?"

How is it possible in this day and age to not have a fax machine? Do they also treat patients with leeches? Am I calling them on their telegraph?

"We don't have a fax machine," the woman repeats cheerfully.

"But…" I sputter. "The last two people I talked to said they were faxing the records over!"

"Faxing or *sending*?" she asks me. "We generally mail out medical records."

Holy crap. Are they serious? They really expect me to wait like five to seven days to get the records on Mrs. Rogers? This is the most ridiculous thing I've ever heard. The smell will surely have killed her by then.

"Do you want me to mail those out to you?" she asks.

"No, don't bother," I say.

I go find Alyssa to report on the situation to her. One thing I know is that at least this isn't my fault. I did my best to get those records. I called three times. They don't have a fax machine—surely she can't blame me for that.

I locate Alyssa in the resident lounge and explain the situation with Mrs. Rogers. I watch her rolling her eyes and I have a really bad feeling. "There's nothing I can do," I insist. "They don't even own a fax machine. Can you believe that?"

"Nothing you can do," Alyssa repeats. "Is that really true, Jane? Is there absolutely nothing you can do to get those records?"

"Uh…" I really wrack my brain, trying to think of a possible way to get the records. It mostly involves some sort of telepathy. "I don't… think so…"

"Think harder," Alyssa says. "How could you get those records rather than just throwing up your hands and giving up?"

When it becomes clear that I have no idea how to answer the question, Alyssa finally takes pity on me and clues me in: "You can go to the nursing home and pick up the records yourself."

I can?

"I'm allowed to leave the hospital?" I ask her. "You said I can *never* leave the hospital while on call."

Alyssa shakes her head. "Well, *I'm* here to cover you. And the nursing home is only five blocks away."

So it is.

It's actually a huge relief to get to leave the hospital. I toss my white coat in the lounge, rescuing only my badge, my pager, and the release of information for Jean Rogers. I figure I'll look like an idiot walking around the streets of Manhattan in a long white coat. Plus, it's about a million degrees out and super muggy.

I take my time walking over to the nursing home. I never ever get to leave the hospital while on duty, so now I'm really milking it. I know the first thing Alyssa will ask when I get back will be, "What took you so long?" But it's worth it.

Maybe I'll get a hot dog.

The nursing home is a dreary place with the dirtiest front steps I've ever seen. It looks like at least one animal and/or person has peed on them. The awning of the building is covered with bird poop, and has long rips in it. The lettering in the sign "Nursing Home" is worn away at the edge, so that it just says "Nursing Ho."

Nursing Ho. Heh.

I march through the entrance, clutching the information release form in my sweaty hand. I'd been hoping for a burst of air conditioning to greet me inside, but instead I realize it's even hotter inside than outside. I wipe away a few strands of sweaty hair that are stuck to the back of my neck.

I scan the corridor of the dreary building, hoping to locate someone who could help me. I see there's a front desk, so I move in that direction, my clogs squeaking loudly on the floor. There's a middle-aged woman sitting there, fanning herself as she talks animatedly to a youngish guy wearing blue scrubs.

The guy in scrubs is carrying a giant cake with the lettering: "Happy Birthday Dad!"

That's kind of sweet, coming to surprise your dad with a big cake like that. What a nice guy.

"Jane?"

I look up from the cake, and surprise surprise!, I'm face to face with none other than Sexy Surgeon. I stare at him, unsure what to say. What the hell is he doing here? I can't imagine *he* was sent here to retrieve records on a patient. And what's the deal with that cake he's holding?

"Hi," I say.

We're still just staring at each other. He isn't volunteering the reason why he's here, and I'm too stunned to say anything to him.

It's pretty awkward until the woman at the desk barks, "Can I help you, Miss?"

"Oh," I say. "Um, I'm trying to get the medical records on a patient of mine."

The woman gives me a dirty look, which is a stark contrast from the googly eyes she was making at Ryan a minute ago. Sometimes I'd love to be a hot surgeon guy.

"We can't just *give* you patient records," she says, folding her arms across her chest. "You need a release to be filled out."

Triumphantly, I hold the signed release in the air. Jean Rogers is pretty demented, but not so much that she can't sign her name, thank God.

"Fine," the woman grumbles and gives me a set of

hasty and confusing directions to get me to medical records.

"Thank you," I say.

I glance over at Ryan, who is still clutching the cake, still with that deer-in-headlights expression. I know he isn't about to tell me why he's here, and I'm betting that by the time I emerge from medical records, he's going to be long gone.

27

I'M TOTALLY RIGHT ABOUT RYAN VANISHING FROM THE nursing home. I make a quick pass through the first floor on my way out and he's nowhere to be found.

What the hell was he doing in a nursing home? And what was up with that cake?

The most obvious answer is that his dad is a resident of the nursing home and he's bringing him a cake for his birthday. But that seems kind of unlikely, somehow. I mean, Ryan's only maybe in his early thirties, tops. How old could his father possibly be? 60? 65? That's way too young to be a resident in a nursing home.

Or maybe the cake wasn't from Ryan, but was from a patient's family member. Maybe Ryan's big secret is that he volunteers in a nursing home on his days off. Despite his assholish exterior, he's really a saint who reads to old people with failing vision. And he didn't want to tell me because he doesn't want to ruin his tough guy façade.

No, that doesn't seem very likely.

Ryan really does seem like an asshole. I can't imagine him having the patience to volunteer with old people. Plus that would be such a cliché.

But then what on earth was he doing at that nursing home? It's driving me crazy! Especially the fact that he seemed so uncomfortable about it and clearly didn't want me to know why he was there.

When I get back into the hospital, I immediately get accosted by a man who's looking for the outpatient pharmacy. I keep insisting I don't know where it is and he keeps insisting I must know, until I finally just point in the opposite direction of where I'm going. I swear, being a doctor is starting to make me dislike human beings.

Unfortunately, Mrs. Rogers's nursing home records are not terribly enlightening. I flip through the pages, searching for any mention of weird or mysterious smells. Nobody has made a note of anything like that.

Right now, in the battle of me versus Mrs. Rogers's body odor, the BO is definitely winning. Has anyone ever published a case report about an atypical case of horrible, mutant BO?

As I head upstairs to report to Alyssa that I have failed to learn absolutely anything new, I practically smack into Ryan at the elevators. His head is clearly somewhere else because he appears to be just as shocked as I am.

"Oh," he says. "Jane."

"Hi," I say.

Neither of us makes a motion to press a button for the elevator. "So," he mumbles, scratching his short blond hair. "That was… a coincidence, I guess. Huh."

"Yeah," I say.

He's avoiding eye contact. I've never seen him do that before. Sexy Surgeon is the master of eye contact.

"My dad works there," he says. "It's his birthday, so, you know, I brought him some cake."

"I thought you said your dad was a lawyer."

Ryan is quiet for a moment. Finally, he says, "Yeah, he's a lawyer for the nursing home."

"The nursing home has its own lawyer?"

"Sure, why not?"

Well, it *is* a pretty crappy nursing home—they could probably use a lawyer. Although it seems doubtful that place could afford an on-site attorney. They can't even afford air conditioning.

"Okay," I say. "Um, in that case, happy birthday to your dad."

"Thanks," Ryan says. "I'll tell him you said so."

I don't know if Ryan planned to take the elevator, but it's clear he doesn't want to be in a confined space with me right now so he takes off for the stairs. I have no idea what Ryan Reilly is hiding, but I'm willing to bet anything that he wasn't at that nursing home to

celebrate the birthday of his dad, the nursing home
lawyer.

28

"Ooh," Kali says. "Maybe he's doing some undercover work there. Maybe he has a whole secret identity!"

Kali and I are taking advantage of our first day off in God knows how long to try to sort out the mystery of what Ryan was doing at that nursing home. It felt so luxurious to wake up without an alarm, and to not have to drag myself to the hospital. I almost don't know what to do with myself.

We ended up in my room because Kali apparently owns the most allergenic cat that ever lived. Everything in her apartment was coated in a thin layer of cat hairs. I never had cat allergies before, but after five minutes in Kali's room, my eyes were watering and my nose was itching. I told her I was going to asphyxiate if I stayed there another minute. She was a little offended, but agreed to relocate.

"I don't think Ryan has a secret identity," I say. "I

don't think he has *time* to have a secret identity. He practically lives in the hospital."

"Maybe he's getting drugs from the nursing home," Kali suggests. "Ooh, maybe he uses the cake to smuggle drugs!"

I roll my eyes. "You think Ryan is a drug addict?"

"Maybe he just sells them," she says. "You have to admit, there's quite a market at County."

She's right about that last part. But I can't imagine Ryan selling drugs. He's worked too hard to get where he is to screw it up like that. Anyway, it's not like he lives large. His only attire is scrubs, and as far as I can tell, he seems to subsist solely on beef jerky and pizza.

"Well," Kali says. "What do *you* think it is?"

I've put a lot of thought into this. And there's only one really reasonable explanation that occurs to me.

"I think the cake really was for his dad," I say. "I think maybe his dad has some menial job at the nursing home, like a janitor or something, and… he's ashamed."

It makes a lot of sense. Ryan acts like he's such hot shit, and he wouldn't want anyone to know if his dad had a job that was any less important than his own.

"Maybe," Kali says thoughtfully. "That or he's smuggling drugs."

I stick out my tongue at her, and she throws a pillow in my direction, giggling. "We should have a pillow fight," she says.

"A what?" I must have heard wrong.

"A pillow fight!" Kali whacks me in the shoulder

with a pillow and I shield myself. "Come on, it will be fun."

"I'm sorry, but no," I say. "I think that we are at the age where the only place it would be appropriate to have a pillow fight would be in pornography."

Kali flops down against my bed, pouting. "Well, what are we supposed to do then? Come on, this is our golden weekend. I don't want to waste it."

In most hospitals, a golden weekend refers to the one weekend of the month where you get both days off. In other words, a golden weekend is just a normal weekend to most people. However, the way the call schedule is set up at our hospital, having both days off is impossible. So the golden weekend just means you get *one* of the two weekend days off. This is actually a rare enough event that it's worth celebrating. But just for the record, our golden weekend isn't even as good as a normal weekend to most people.

"It's not really a golden weekend," I point out. "It's more like… a silver weekend."

"It's a day that I'm not in the hospital," Kali says. "Which makes it pretty damn special."

Our conversation is interrupted by banging on my door. I struggle to my feet and go to answer it. Naturally, it's my roommate, Julia. Her hair is still in that uber-tight ponytail and she does not look happy.

"You have an unauthorized visitor," Julia says, glaring across my room at Kali.

"It's just Kali," I say.

"I didn't give my approval," Julia says. "Plus you

have to give me 24 hours' notice."

"Are you shitting me?" Kali says.

Kali and Julia are glowering at each other. I feel compelled to at least attempt to make some sort of peace between the two of them.

"Come on, Julia," I say. "It's our day off. Why don't you come join us?"

Kali seems horrified, but for a moment, Julia actually looks like she's considering it. But then she stiffens and shakes her head.

"I'm busy studying," she says. She looks me up and down critically. "You should be studying too. I overheard Alyssa complaining to another resident that you never do any reading and have no idea what you're doing."

Why am I not surprised?

"We're going out now anyway," Kali says, jutting her chin out in Julia's direction. "I just came by to have a look at how disgusting your bathroom was."

Okay, yes, I did tell Kali about the Bathroom Manifesto. And Julia looks pretty wounded at the mention of her bathroom being any less than spotless. But I have to say, she kind of had this coming. I actually feel a twinge of satisfaction as we brush past her on our way out the door.

I'm locking the door to the suite when I hear Kali gasp slightly. I look up and there he is: Sexy Surgeon. Wearing real clothes: jeans and a T-shirt. His hair is sticking up slightly and he looks pretty tired, but of course, still sexy. "Ryan," I murmur.

Ryan glances at Kali, then back at me. "Jane, can we talk?"

Kali's eyes widen—she gets the hint immediately. "I've got to go give Val her shot now, actually," she says. "Um, I'll see you later, Jane."

Kali scurries down the hallway, and Ryan watches her go. He frowns. "Who's Val?"

"Her cat." I add, "He has diabetes."

"Right," Ryan murmurs. He couldn't care less. He jerks his head in the direction of my door. "Can we go inside?"

I hesitate. Julia said not to, but I'm hoping she's gotten the crazy out of her system for the day. Anyway, I saw Ryan yelling at her in the hallway the other day for an inappropriate consult, so I suspect she's a little bit afraid of him right now. I don't think she'll bother us.

"Sure," I say.

Inside my room, we both settle down on my bed. But it's clear that there isn't going to be any sexy time right now. Ryan sits about three feet away from me, and he does not appear to be in an amorous mood. His usually ramrod-straight spine is slumped over and he's staring down at his hands. I don't say anything. I'm afraid that if I say the wrong thing, he might change his mind about telling me.

"My father isn't a nursing home lawyer," he finally says.

Yeah, no kidding.

"I'm sorry I lied to you," he adds.

"It's okay," I say. I want to reach over and take his hand, but he's just a little too far away. "Whatever he does for a living, there's no shame in that."

Ryan lifts his head. His brow is furrowed. "What do you mean?"

"I mean," I say, "there's no shame in cleaning toilets or... or, you know, whatever it is your father does."

He shakes his head. "Jane, my father isn't a janitor at the nursing home." He averts his eyes again. "He's a resident."

"Oh," I say.

That's odd. I did think of that, of course, but immediately rejected the idea, because Ryan's father is probably only...

"He's 64," Ryan says, completing my thought.

"Oh," I say again. Apparently, that's the only thing I'm capable of saying anymore.

"Jane," he says. "You can't tell anyone about this, okay? You swear, right?"

"Of course," I say.

He inspects my face for a minute and I try to look as truthful as possible.

Finally, he says, "He has Huntington's Disease."

In medical school, you end up learning a few facts about practically every disease there is. Like there's this disease where your urine smells like maple syrup. For real. I've never seen anyone with that disease and surely never will, but I could name at least three facts about patients with maple syrup urine disease.

Huntington's Disease is relatively rare and not something I've ever seen before. But I learned about it and could recite three facts about it. First, it's a severe neurodegenerative disease where you get something called chorea, meaning large, involuntary movements of the extremities. Second, the patients usually get a cognitive decline that evolves into dementia starting at around age 40, which I guess is why Ryan's father is in a nursing home. And third…

"Ryan," I say, "isn't Huntington's disease…?"

He nods. "Autosomal dominant."

The mutation that causes Huntington's Disease occurs on a single gene. Every person has two copies of every gene, one from each parent. If a disease is "autosomal recessive," that means you need two copies of the gene in order to be affected. If the disease is "autosomal dominant," however, that means you need only one abnormal copy.

In practical terms, what that means is that if your parent has an autosomal dominant disease, you have a 50% chance of getting it yourself.

Oh my God.

"Do…" My voice comes out squeaky. I clear my throat. "Do you have the gene?"

Ryan shakes his head. "I don't know."

I cock my head at him. "I thought you could be tested for it?"

"Yeah, you can," he confirms. "But I'm not interested. I don't want to know."

"Seriously?" I stare at him. "But… isn't it driving

you crazy not to know? I mean, what if you don't have it?"

"Jane," he sighs. "Listen, I've thought about it. A lot. But here's the thing. My sister got tested and she was negative. She's happy now, has a job, a husband, and two kids. A great life." He looks back down at his hands. "My brother got tested and was positive. He's now an alcoholic, and he lives in his car. That's if his car hasn't been impounded."

I see what he's saying, I suppose. But to me, it seems worth the risk. How could you go through life without knowing?

"I've got a 50% shot of having it," he says. "I can live with that. I can still go through my life, enjoy my job, and do everything I want to do more or less with that 50% chance. If it were 100%... I'm not sure if I could. I can't take that risk—50% is the most I can deal with."

"But it's irresponsible," I blurt out. "I mean, what about when you get married and have kids?"

He smiles crookedly at me. "Well, I'm not going to do those things, so it's not a problem."

"Are you serious?"

He nods. "I *can't.* I can't take the chance of passing it on to another person, so… I'm not going to start a family. No kids. You're right—it would be irresponsible. Even if I didn't pass it on, my father started having symptoms in his early forties. That's too young to lose your father. I should know."

I can't believe what I'm hearing.

"If you knew you didn't have the gene," I say, "would you get married and have kids then?"

"Yeah," he says, his voice heavy. "I would. But…" He looks up at me with those deep blue eyes. "I love being a surgeon, Jane. I love my job, I really do. And that's enough for me."

"I don't know," I say. "I think you should get tested. Imagine how great it would be if you turned out to be negative. Right?"

Ryan frowns. "Seriously, don't try to talk me into it. I've been dealing with this decision for twenty years. I promise you, you're not going to change my mind." He slides over a foot on the bed, close enough that he can put his hand on mine. "If you really want to help me, then just promise me you won't tell anyone else."

"Of course I won't." I raise my eyebrows. "Nobody else knows?"

He shakes his head. "I don't want people to look at me funny. And I definitely don't want pity."

No, he just wants to be the asshole surgeon. But I get it. He doesn't want to be treated any differently. He wants to earn respect, just like everyone else.

Ryan envelops my fingers in his. "I'm glad I told you, Jane. I've been keeping this to myself for so long… it feels really good to finally tell someone. Get it off my chest, you know?"

He starts kissing me, pushing me down onto the bed, his hands lacing into my hair, which is loose for a change. I can't help but think about the fact that Ryan doesn't have the luxury of falling in love. No matter how much he cares about a woman, he can never be with her for more than a short term relationship. He'll never have a family. He'll never have some little kid looking up to him and calling him Daddy, even though I can see in his eyes that he wants that. He has to give up so damn much.

It's so unfair.

Ryan pulls away from me, and studies my face. "Jane, are you *crying*?"

I wipe my eyes. "No. I mean, maybe just a little."

"What the hell?" he snaps.

I grab a tissue from the box that's next to my bed. "I just… I feel bad…"

Ryan jumps up off the bed, glaring at me. "You're kidding me, right? This is *exactly* why I haven't told anyone about this."

"Sorry," I mumble.

His blue eyes meet mine. "You don't need to feel sorry for me."

"I don't," I lie.

He knows I'm full of it though. He shakes his head at me, and storms out of my room, slamming the door behind him. I guess that's the end of me and Sexy Surgeon.

Hours awake: 4
Chance of Sexy Surgeon dying young of a neurode-generative disease: 50%

As I'm waiting for the elevator to go into the hospital, a mother and her little girl pass by. The girl says to her mom, "Look, Mommy! A doctor!"

She meant me. How cute.

Things go downhill after that.

I discover that on my day off, Mrs. Jefferson developed a fever and her white blood cells are elevated. She was supposed to finally go home tomorrow, but now it looks like that plan is at least temporarily on hold.

Just my luck. I mean, just *her* luck.

There's already an admission waiting for us from the night service. I meet Alyssa in the resident lounge to get sign-out from the overnight resident who did the admission. She looks decidedly pissed off when she sees me. But what else is new?

"How come you didn't do the discharge paperwork on Mrs. Rogers?" she demands to know. "She went home yesterday and I had to write her discharge while covering both your patients and Connie's."

"Mrs. Rogers was discharged?" I'm shocked. As of two days ago, she looked like she was practically dead. Well, she *smelled* dead, at least.

Alyssa just shakes her head at me. "In the future, if you know a patient is going home on your day off, you need to do the discharge summary in advance."

I also need to develop psychic abilities, apparently.

"Sorry." I can't help but ask, "Did you ever figure out why she smelled so bad?"

Alyssa looks horrified by my question. "*Excuse* me?"

"Well, she had that smell," I say, "and it was really bad, like the whole hallway smelled horrible, and nobody knew why…" I stop short, aware that Alyssa is glaring at me. "Never mind," I mumble.

I guess I'll never find out what that smell was. Damn.

"Also, Mr. Dugan had a headache this morning," she says. "I wrote an order for some ibuprofen for him."

"Actually," I say, "that's probably not the medication I'd pick, considering he's got renal insufficiency."

Alyssa gets quiet for a minute. Finally, she says, "Yes, that's true. Switch it to Tylenol."

Score! Alyssa actually admitted I was right about something. This may never happen again. I need to savor it. Ahhh.

I hear a loud whirring noise coming from

outside and a large scooter navigates into the lounge. Sitting atop the scooter is a resident named Jim, who was the senior admitting overflow patients last night. Why he's sitting on a scooter is beyond me. I saw him no less than a week ago darting around the hospital on his own two feet. This is just bizarre.

"Jesus Christ," I say. "What happened to you?"

Jim's face lights up, clearly loving the attention of zipping around in a scooter. "You won't believe this," he begins. "So you know that big dumpster behind the hospital…"

Alyssa clears her throat loudly. "I'm sorry but we don't have time to socialize right now. Could you just tell us about the patient, please?"

"Spoilsport," Jim grumbles as he fumbles through the papers in the basket on his scooter. Seriously, this is so weird. And what did Jim do in that dumpster that landed him in a scooter? "Aha, here we go. The patient is Richard Thurman, 38 years old. At about 4 a.m., he was FOOBA."

I frown. "FOOBA?"

Jim winks at me. "Found On Ortho, Barely Alive. The guy had a severe traumatic brain injury from a motorcycle crash, but orthopedic surgery was keeping him to nail his femur fracture. He was looking pretty puny last night, going in and out of a-fib, his blood pressure all over the place, his blood sugars completely uncontrolled. He's still pretty sick, so you better keep a close eye on him."

Alyssa does not look pleased. "Maybe he'd be better off in the ICU if he's that sick."

"Nah," Jim says. "Frankly, his worst problem is that he's FOS."

I raise my eyebrows. "FOS?"

"Full of shit." Jim snickers and my heart skips a beat. Please don't let me have to do a stool disimpaction. "Don't worry, Jane. I threw some Mag Citrate at him and I think most of it came out."

Thank God.

After Jim zips away on his scooter, Alyssa and I go to pay Mr. Thurman a visit. When we see him, it's pretty clear that his femur fracture is the least of his problems. Whatever happened to his brain was pretty bad. He's two months out from the injury, and essentially in a minimally conscious state. His eyes look in two different directions and his only actions are to try to pull at his tubes, which is why his arms are in restraints. He has a long scar along the left side of his scalp and underneath a large chunk of his skull seems to be missing.

Per his chart, Mr. Thurman was in a motorcycle accident and he wasn't wearing a helmet. I'm not a risk taker and I've always thought motorcycles were scary dangerous. I mean, cars have a ton of metal protecting you, and then airbags on top of that, but when it's a motorcycle, there's nothing but air between you and the other cars (or the ground or a tree). So it seems like the least you could do is protect your skull with a helmet. But not everyone feels that way, apparently.

I've heard that motorcycle riders have lobbied against helmet laws, saying it's a violation of their rights. What I don't understand is why wouldn't you *want* to wear a helmet if you were on a motorcycle? What excuse could you possibly have? It's uncomfortable? It makes you look uncool?

Believe me, if pre-injury Mr. Thurman could see the way he looks right now, he would not be pleased.

Alyssa gives me the all-important job of tracking down exactly how much poop has come out of Mr. Thurman this morning. But before she goes, she has one final set of words of wisdom for me.

"By the way," she says. "Mrs. Jefferson had an elevated white blood count two days ago. You missed it."

I stare at her. "What? I didn't miss anything."

Alyssa nods. "You did. The labs you wrote down in your note for that day were from the day before."

I pause for a second, contemplating how this mistake could have happened. The answer is: easily. I saw a set of labs and wrote them down, not bothering to double check the date on them. I can just see how I might have done it.

Of course, half of Alyssa's job is to look at labs. Sometimes I catch her in the computer lab, just sitting there reviewing labs for large chunks of time. So the missed lab was as much her fault as mine.

Maybe even *more* her fault than mine.

But I don't say that. Instead, I say, "I'll culture her and start antibiotics."

———

I'VE NOTICED the nurses don't particularly like me. It's not that they dislike me, but they definitely don't *like* me even though I'm fairly polite and respectful to them. Here's the thing: if you were doing a job for over twenty years and then some 25 year old came in and you were expected to take orders from her, how much would you like that person? Not a whole lot, that's how much.

Unless, of course, that person was incredibly handsome, like a certain surgery resident I could name.

A nurse named Patti flags me down on the telemetry floor in the afternoon and has a pile of annoying questions for me.

"Doctor," she says. "I need to talk to you about the new patient Mrs. Levy."

"Okay," I say, bracing myself.

"We need to open up a bed on this floor," she says. "Mrs. Levy already had two sets of cardiac enzymes that were negative, so can we move her to the regular floor?"

"What about the third set I ordered?" I ask.

"We didn't draw it," she admits.

I raise my eyebrows.

"It wouldn't be back yet anyway!" Patti says.

"Well, it definitely won't be back if you never draw it."

Patti just glares at me. But seriously, she knows I'm right. The rule is three sets of negative cardiac enzymes before they can leave telemetry.

"Also," she says, "Mr. Gregory in room 204 wants to eat."

That's a patient I'm cross-covering so I check the sign-out. He's supposed to have surgery today, which means he can't eat.

"Sorry," I say. "He's NPO for surgery."

"But he's really hungry," Patti whines.

I want to ask her if this is a serious question. I'm sure Ryan would be screaming at her by now. Actually, he wouldn't, because she wouldn't dare ask him such a dumb question.

I glance down again at the sign-out for Mr. Gregory to see if they've added any helpful hints. In addition to the note about the surgery, the resident had typed: "If patient is agitated, give him a dose of fativan."

*Fat*ivan? As far as I know, there is no such medication. There is, however, a sedative called Ativan. Presumably, the intern meant Ativan, which calms you down. Unless he really meant *fat*ivan, which… I don't know, makes you fat? Or less fat?

"You can give him some Ativan," I say generously.

Patti nods, somewhat placated.

I get a page and hurry off to answer it. It turns out that now Mrs. Jefferson is having chest pain. She's never leaving us. Welcome to your home forever: County Hospital.

Hours awake: 5
Chance of Mrs. Jefferson getting to go home this week: 15% and falling

30

"It's been coming on all morning," Mrs. Jefferson explains to me. "And I feel like it's a bit hard to breathe, you know?"

Mrs. Jefferson's EKG is normal. I'm waiting for the chest X-ray to show up online, but she doesn't look that bad. She just looks worried. Thomas Jefferson is sitting at her bedside, holding her hand, looking equally worried.

"You're going to be okay," I promise her. "You get angina, right?"

"Not like this," she says.

I nod. "Okay, well, we're going to do a bunch of tests, wait for your labs to come back, but I don't really think anything bad is going on."

"I believe you, Dr. Jane," she says. "I know you always do a really good job. I know you're looking out for me."

I feel a stab of guilt about missing that elevated

white blood count the other day. But she doesn't need to know about that.

I make it out of the room and as far as the nurses' station before Thomas Jefferson catches up with me. He's got a crease between his eyebrows. "Dr. Jane, I'm worried about my Markie."

"I understand," I say in my most understanding voice. "She's going to be okay. We're going to get to the bottom of this."

"You don't get it," he says. "Through this whole ordeal, no matter how bad things got, she always told me everything was going to be fine. But today she didn't say that. She said to me that she thought she was never gonna leave this hospital."

"I'm sure that's just because she was so close to going home," I say. "And I promise you, she *will* go home."

Thomas Jefferson looks skeptical.

"I promise you," I say again.

"Okay," he finally says. "I believe you, Dr. Jane."

I watch him walk back into his wife's room. I feel good about the fact that I reassured him. One thing I've been realizing lately is that people bounce back pretty easily if you give them a chance. Mrs. Jefferson is sick today, but I feel certain she'll be going home soon. Thomas Jefferson isn't a doctor (he's a Founding Father), so he just doesn't know that.

I locate Alyssa in the radiology reading room. She's flipping through X-rays done on our patients from the last few days. "Hey," I say. "Is Mrs. Jefferson's chest X-ray up yet?"

Alyssa nods. "Yeah, I just looked at it. It's negative."

"Oh," I say, disappointed. A pneumonia would have given us an explanation for her fevers. "Can I see it?"

Alyssa whirls around with her classic "why are you wasting my time" expression.

"Never mind," I quickly say. It's far too early in the call to be pissing off Alyssa.

———

FOR THE FIRST time all month, the call is going smoothly. It's a miracle.

I've got all my admissions tucked away by midnight, and I manage to retire to my call room before 1 a.m. I might even get a full night of sleep while on call. I actually seem to be getting the hang of this whole doctor thing.

At 1:45 a.m., things start to fall apart.

My pager goes off and I know before I even answer it that it's about Mr. Thurman. He's been tottering on the brink of something awful all day, and it makes sense that he waited for the very moment I fell asleep to start crumping. "Hello, this is Dr. McGill," I say.

"Hi, Doctor," the nurse says. "I'm calling about Mr. Thurman."

Naturally.

"His blood pressure is low," the nurse says. "It's 81 over 53."

"And what are the rest of his vitals?" I ask.

The nurse hesitates. "Um, hang on."

I sigh, but then get freaked out by how much I sounded like Alyssa just now. I start getting my shoes on because no matter what the nurse tells me, I'm going to be heading over to see Mr. Thurman. I expect he's going to make a journey to the ICU tonight.

After the nurse reports back to me, I tell her I'm on my way, then I page Alyssa to let her know. "Mr. Thurman's really sick," Alyssa says. No kidding. "I'm going to call the ICU and see if they're willing to take him. He's probably going to need some pressure support. Does he have a central line?"

"No," I say.

Alyssa swears under her breath, then hangs up the phone.

By the time I get to Mr. Thurman's bedside, he isn't looking good. His oxygen levels are dropping and his blood pressure is still low. I check the chart and confirm that he's Full Code. Meaning we have to do everything possible to save the guy's life, even though it's not clear he'll ever have any real quality of life ever again. It seems, in all honesty, like a bit of a waste. But I'm not going to argue the point right now.

It's probably a blessing at this point that Mr. Thurman doesn't really appear to know what's going on. His head is lolling around and he grunts a few times as sweat breaks out on his forehead. The reading on the monitor tells me his blood pressure is still dropping.

Alyssa materializes at the bedside and I feel nothing but relief. "Should we put in a central line?" I ask her.

She bites her lip. "I can't. I'm not signed off yet."

In order for a resident to be allowed to do a procedure independently, they have to be observed a certain number of times by an attending physician. At that point, they are "signed off" to do the procedure. Apparently, Alyssa hasn't reached that level of skill with placing central lines.

"What about the ICU resident?" I ask.

Alyssa shakes her head. "She's a junior. She's done less than I have."

Well, great. I guess we're just going to have to let him die then.

"Call Surgery," Alyssa says to me.

"Huh?" I say.

She grits her teeth. "Get the person on call for Surgery. They'll put in a line. They're great at it."

"Okay," I mumble.

I know before I even speak to the operator that she's going to tell me that Dr. Reilly is on call for Surgery tonight because that is the kind of luck I've been having. I page him and sit by the phone, waiting for the call back. I don't expect him to return the page. He never does.

So I'm pretty shocked when the phone rings: "This is Dr. Reilly, returning a page."

"Hi," I say. "Um, it's Jane."

Ryan is quiet for a minute. "Why are you paging me?"

"We've got a guy who needs a central line… urgently."

He sighs. "Don't you have a senior resident?"

"She's not signed off," I explain.

Ryan snorts. "What do they teach you guys over there, anyway?"

"Come on," I say. "Please… just help us out…" Help *me* out.

There's a long pause on the other line while I hold my breath.

"Yeah, fine," he says. "I'll be there in five."

I expect him to take his sweet time getting over here, but once again Ryan Reilly manages to surprise me. A few minutes later, he arrives on the ward carrying a central line kit. He doesn't look me in the eyes, and when he addresses me, it's in a sharp monotone. Like I'm just some intern he's never met before. "Where's the patient?" he asks.

I lead him to Mr. Thurman's room. He eyes the patient, with his wonky pupils, the drool pooling in the corner of his mouth, and the feeding tube in his belly.

"Jesus," Ryan says. "What's wrong with him?"

"Brain injury," I say. "Motorcycle accident."

Ryan shakes his head. "Maybe this is God telling you something…"

I stare at him. "What are you saying?"

His eyes finally meet mine. "You don't think this is all a huge waste?"

"No, I don't," I say angrily. Although to be honest, I really sort of do. But I don't want him to win this argument. "I mean, if it were you or your family member…"

"If it were *me*," Ryan interrupts, "it would be over *right now*. Hell, *way* before now." He glares at Mr. Thurman, as if he is furious at the man for having the gall to be alive. "That will never be me. *Never*."

I don't like what Ryan is saying. I swallow hard. "Look, can you put in the line, please?"

He nods curtly before gowning up to go inside the room. I've only seen a handful of central lines placed in my short medical career, but it's obvious Ryan is very experienced with them. His hands are incredibly steady as he slips the catheter into place and slides out the guidewire. It takes only a few minutes, which is a good thing considering I'm practically holding my breath the whole time.

Ryan pulls his gloves off with a loud snap as he pushes past me out of the room. "Congratulations," he says. "Your patient lives another day."

I watch him as he grabs the patient's chart to scribble a quick note about how he came in to save the day. I want to say something to him, apologize somehow, but I'm pretty sure anything I say will come out wrong. If I compliment the work he just did, he'll think I'm patronizing him. Anyway, I'm sure he doesn't think he did anything so spectacular just now. He's a surgeon. Putting in central lines is probably like breathing to him.

As I wrack my brain to think of what I can say, I hear a loud voice booming overhead: "Code Blue in Room 327B. Code Blue in Room 327B."

I'm not on the code team tonight so my first instinct is to ignore it. Then I remember: Mrs. Jefferson is in Room 327B. And then I run.

Hours awake: 20
Chance of Mrs. Jefferson living till morning: ?????????

31

It's clear I'm one of the last to arrive. The room is packed with the code team and there's a nurse inside who is pumping on Mrs. Jefferson's chest, her massive body bouncing with each compression.

I race over, yelling, "She's my patient! What happened?"

Naturally, nobody answers. And that's when I see Thomas Jefferson, standing outside the room, wringing his hands together and tugging on his funny little beard.

"Dr. Jane," he says quietly. His eyes are filled with fear.

I wince. I promised him less than 24 hours ago that his wife would be fine. Now I can see them preparing to intubate her. She's so far from fine, it's not even funny.

"What happened?" I ask him.

"I came to bring her a snack," he says, holding up a brown paper sack. "And I couldn't wake her up."

"Still no pulse!" I hear someone yell from within the room.

Oh God. She's going to die. Somehow at that moment, I know it with absolute certainty. I look over at Thomas Jefferson and I realize that he knows it too.

"Can you stop this, Dr. Jane?" he asks me. "Markie wouldn't want all these people here. She'd just want to go quietly."

I nod. "Is that what *you* want?"

Thomas Jefferson's brow creases and I see the tears welling up in his eyes. "Yes, please."

I close my eyes and brace myself as I walk into the room. The senior resident is attempting to intubate her, and she's still flatline on the monitor. I walk over to the resident who seems to be running the code and tap him on the shoulder.

"Hey," I say.

The resident barely glances at me. With a shaking hand, he's holding up a cheat sheet of medications that can be used during a code. I've got an identical one in my pocket.

"What is it?" he asks in a distracted voice.

"Her husband wants us to stop the code," I say.

The resident turns back to me and I can see the relief flood his features.

"Oh, okay," he says. He addresses the crowd surrounding Mrs. Jefferson, which is substantial. There are so many people doing so many things to her that her body still seems to be in motion. "I'm calling the code. Husband wants us to stop."

And just like that, it's over.

I leave the room with everyone else, my heart still pounding in my chest. I see the miniscule Thomas Jefferson watching everyone exit his wife's room. He catches me before I can get past him.

"Thank you, Dr. Jane," he says, although I don't know what he's thanking me for. I told him his wife was going to be all right and I was wrong. I let her die. I screwed up. I definitely don't deserve to be thanked.

I don't say any of that though. I just nod.

He glances into the room. "Can I hold her hand as she goes?"

"Go ahead," I say, even though the reality is that she's already gone.

Mr. Thomas Jefferson goes back into the room and sits at his wife's bedside. Her gown has been pulled down by the code team and he gently rights it for her. He picks her limp hand off the bed and strokes her smooth, unlined face with his other hand. With her eyes closed, she seems so peaceful.

"It's all over, Markie," he says gently. He brushes away a strand of hair that has fallen in her face. "All your suffering is finally over. You're free."

I watch them for another minute before I race to the bathroom just in time to burst into tears.

Hours Awake: Oh, fuck it all to hell

32

A FEW HOURS LATER, WE MEET FOR ROUNDS WITH DR. Westin like nothing happened.

I'm all cried out. My eyes are still puffy but everyone probably thinks it's from lack of sleep. Nobody would believe I was actually crying over *a patient*. Even Thomas Jefferson has no idea. I was too embarrassed to face him again. In my head, I keep replaying that moment when I told him that his wife would be fine, that she'd definitely go home with him.

I *promised* him.

Alyssa sits next to me in Dr. Westin's office. She's got a list of all our patients in front of her and she's drawn a line through the name Marquette Jefferson.

As usual, Connie goes through her patients before I do. She's only got two of them left so it goes quickly. Then it's my turn.

"My, my, my, unfortunate business last night," Dr.

Westin says to me. "You're quite the black cloud, aren't you, Jackie?"

A "black cloud" refers to a person who generally has bad luck on calls. I think the term could accurately be applied to my entire internship so far.

"Yep," is what I say.

"Very unfortunate," Dr. Westin muses.

I wish he'd just move on. Alyssa has already drawn a line through her name—why can't we talk about something else before I start crying again?

"What did Surgery say about the pneumothorax?" Dr. Westin asks.

I blink at him. "What? What pneumothorax?"

A pneumothorax occurs when air gets into the space between the lung and the chest wall. It can potentially collapse the lung, so if it's bad enough, Surgery can stick in a needle or a tube to release the air.

But why is Dr. Westin talking about a pneumothorax?

"It was on Mrs. Jefferson's chest X-ray," he says. "Wasn't it? Here, let me bring it up on my computer."

I practically leap off my chair to get a closer look at the computer screen. Within seconds, a picture of Mrs. Jefferson's chest cavity fills the monitor.

And there it is, on the upper right side: a very clear pneumothorax. A vein starts to throb in my temple.

"I see it!" Connie chirps. "It's on the right."

"She had a PICC line put in recently, didn't she?" Dr. Westin muses. "That probably did it."

I jerk my head up to look at Alyssa, who is silent. Not acknowledging the fact that *she* was the one who misread the X-ray as negative.

And now that patient is dead.

My eyes fall again on her list of patients, at Mrs. Jefferson's name crossed off the list. Like she's *nothing*. Like her death didn't even *matter*. All the awful things Alyssa's said to me this month flash through my brain until I start seeing red. And at that point, I just can't stop myself.

"This is your fault," I hiss at Alyssa. My cheeks feel like they're blazing. "*You* are the one who read the X-ray. You read it wrong! If you were competent at your job, that woman would still be alive right now."

Alyssa stares at me, shocked by my outburst. "Jane, I didn't—"

"Didn't what?" I burst in. "Drop the ball? *Obviously* you did. You talk about high standards and being knowledgeable when it comes to total bullshit, but when it's actually *important* and a person's *life* is at stake, you don't have a *clue* what you're doing. You can't even read a goddamn chest X-ray!"

Alyssa's mouth is open. She looks like she has something to say to me, but she can't get the words out. Good. Because I've got one more thing left to say to her.

"You killed Mrs. Jefferson," I practically spit at her. "You deserve to lose your license."

Everyone sits there in stunned silence for at least 60 seconds. Even I'm sort of stunned, to be perfectly honest. I can't believe I said all that. I was thinking it, but I can't believe I actually said it. But now that I did, I'm glad. She deserved every word of it.

Alyssa rises from her seat. She's taller than I am, and for a second, I'm slightly afraid she might hit me. I sort of deserve it. But she doesn't. Instead she whirls around and storms out of Dr. Westin's office.

We all watch her leave. It's only after she's gone that I get an inkling that I did something kind of inappropriate. What was I *thinking*?

"That," Dr. Westin says, "was incredibly unprofessional."

I hang my head. "I'm sorry."

Dr. Westin considers me for a moment, contemplating my fate. I'm suddenly really embarrassed. Why did I say all that? I'm not five years old. I'm in control of my words. It's not my fault! I'm just really, really tired.

"You need to go apologize to her, Jane," he says.

I nod. I can't believe he finally got my name right. And now he'll remember it forever.

———

I try paging Alyssa but she doesn't answer. That freaks me out a little, because unlike Sexy Surgeon,

Alyssa always answers pages promptly. If she's ignoring her pager, I must have really upset her.

I end up searching the whole damn hospital for Alyssa. She's not in any of the usual locations: the wards, the resident lounge, the call rooms, the cafeteria.

I'm about to give up when I remember that night when I declared that patient dead for the first time and Ryan took me up to the roof. On a whim, I head up to the roof. At the very least, I'll get some fresh air. I could use it.

As the door to the roof swings open, I immediately see her. Alyssa. She's leaning over the edge, facing away from me, holding her phone in her hand. She's not talking to anyone though. She's just looking at the phone. As I get closer, I realize she's looking at a photo of her son.

My chest tightens. She's not going to jump, is she? If I drove her to do that, it's a million times worse than whatever she did or didn't do to Mrs. Jefferson. "Alyssa," I gasp.

She whips her head around. When I see her face, I notice that her eyes are red-rimmed.

"Are you okay?" I say, trying to sound gentle, like the way I'd talk to patients on my psychiatry rotation.

Alyssa snorts and shoves her phone back into her pocket.

"I'm sorry about what I said," I say, taking a careful step towards her. "Just… you know, don't do anything crazy."

Alyssa wipes her eyes. "Don't worry, I'm not going to throw myself off the building, if that's what you're thinking."

"Oh," I say, my shoulders sagging in relief. "Alyssa, I shouldn't have said that you... that you killed Mrs. Jefferson. You didn't."

I'm being honest. Yes, Alyssa missed the pneumothorax. But now that I'm being realistic, that pneumothorax was admittedly pretty small. Mrs. Jefferson was a really sick woman, and as of now, it's not clear that any intervention done for that pneumothorax would have made a difference. In all likelihood, she still would have died. If not today, then tomorrow. It was inevitable—even Mrs. Jefferson realized it.

"No, you had it right the first time," Alyssa says. "I did. I killed her. Or at least, I let her die." She takes a deep breath. "That's something I'm going to have to live with the rest of my life."

I don't know what to say to that.

"I hope it never happens to you," she says.

We stand there in silence for a minute, then Alyssa shivers with a passing breeze. She hugs herself for a moment then pushes past me to go back into the hospital and get back to work.

33

It feels decadent, but I stay on the roof for several minutes after Alyssa leaves. After my meltdown in Dr. Westin's office, I'm pretty sure nobody expects me back quite yet. They're probably debating if they need to call a psychiatry consult on me.

That might not be an entirely terrible idea, actually.

I take Alyssa's place on the edge of the roof, watching all the people milling about on the street. None of these people have any idea that Mrs. Jefferson just died. They don't even know who she is. Why would they?

But I know. And I will always remember.

"Don't jump."

My breath catches in my throat and I whirl around. I should have known: it's Sexy Surgeon. He's standing at the door to the roof, still looking sexy as all hell in his blue scrubs, his short blond hair being tossed every which way by the wind. He's smiling crookedly, which is better than the hateful glare he gave me last time I saw him.

"I wasn't going to jump," I say, shaking my head.

"It's still worth saying," he says, joining me at the edge. He gets close enough that I can feel the heat of his body. "I heard you lost a patient last night. I'm sorry."

I nod. I turn my face away from him so he can't see the tears gathering in my eyes. Why do I keep crying? Nobody else here cries when they lose a patient. It must be the lack of sleep.

"I wish I could be more like you," I say bitterly. "Like, not caring when a patient dies. That would be much easier."

"I care," Ryan insists, his blue eyes wide.

"Yeah, right."

"I do." He hesitates for a moment, then says, "Your patient, Mrs. Coughlin—she died on the operating table right in front of me. The reason I didn't tell you wasn't because I didn't care. I *couldn't* tell you because I felt so awful about it."

I raise my eyebrows, daring to look at him. He seems to be telling the truth.

"The surgeon who operated on her is a complete asshole," he begins.

"Worse than you?"

"Way worse," Ryan says. "You have no idea. Anyway, I thought he missed tying off one of the vessels and I didn't say anything because I was scared he was going to ream me out, and I figured I was probably wrong. Then she bled out and she died." He closes his eyes. "She died right in front of us. It was horrible. And I kept thinking that if only I'd said something, she would have lived." He pauses, and when he opens his eyes again, they're wet. "She was a nice lady. It was hard to tell her family what happened. Really hard."

So the Great Ryan Reilly is actually a human being. Who would have thunk it?

"And," he adds, "I'm sorry I got pissed off at you the other day. I know I dropped a huge bombshell on you and it's unfair that I expected you not to react."

I nod. "It was… surprising."

"I'll bet."

We're both quiet for a minute, staring down at the city below. I can just barely pick out individuals, going about their daily lives. A man hosing off the sidewalk in front of his store. A homeless man shaking a cup of spare change. A lady hailing a cab. Three people waiting for the bus to arrive.

"You know," I say thoughtfully. "I was just realizing that if you do make it to age 50, you're in the clear, right? Probably, I mean."

Ryan narrows his eyes. "Yeah, so?"

"Well," I say. "That means when you're 50, you can go ahead and get married and have kids."

I think of Mrs. Jefferson's husband sitting at her bedside as she passed on, holding her hand. I want

Ryan to have that when he dies. Everyone should have that.

"Great," Ryan snorts. "I'll be the only 60-year-old dad at Little League. Just what I want."

"You'll just have to find some young, trophy wife to marry," I say. "But I'm assuming you'd do that anyway."

"Oh, yeah, of course," Ryan laughs.

"Your future wife probably isn't even in kindergarten yet," I add.

"Hell," Ryan says, "she probably isn't *born* yet."

I warm up to the game: "Her future parents probably haven't even undergone puberty yet."

Ryan laughs again, but then he gets quiet for a minute, staring off into the distance.

"Or maybe you'll be available," he muses. He smiles winningly and I feel his hand slip into mine. "What do you think?"

I roll my eyes. "If you think I'm waiting for you 20 years, think again, buster. You're not *that* good-looking."

"You don't have to wait for me," he says, grinning. "You can just dump whatever loser you're with 20 years from now."

I imagine Ryan Reilly 20 years from now. His blond hair will be threaded with gray and there will be crow's feet around those blue eyes, but I can tell he'll still be incredibly sexy. Maybe even more so. And he'll be a great surgeon by then. Maybe he'll be head of the whole surgical department. He definitely has it in him.

And me? I'll still be Dr. Jane McGill.

Hours awake: Lost track
Chance of a happy ending: At least 50%

EPILOGUE
ONE YEAR LATER

THIS INTERN IS THE DUMBEST INTERN I'VE EVER MET in my life.

Her name is Maddie and I've been her senior resident for exactly two weeks. Two of the longest weeks of my life. At first, I gave her a pass because she was brand new and… well, *I've been there before*. I didn't want to make her cry. There's so much to learn when you're first starting out as a brand new doctor and I didn't want to say anything that would make her take a flying leap off the roof of County Hospital. I don't need *that* on my conscience.

But over the last two weeks, I swear to God, she's getting *dumber*. There are things she seemed to know during the first week that she doesn't seem to know anymore. At the very least, she's not retaining any new information. When I teach her something, it's like throwing a piece of paper into a completely full trash can and just watching it bounce off and roll away.

Right now, we're in the Emergency Room and Maddie is presenting a new patient to me. It's not even midnight yet and already she appears hopelessly frazzled. Her black hair is coming loose from the bun she tied it in, but only on the right side, so the right half of her hair is down and the left side is still up. She's got patient information scribbled all over the right leg of her scrub pants, probably violating all sorts of patient privacy laws. And she's got pit stains. How does she have pit stains? It isn't even that hot in here!

"Mr. Gomez has been coughing for the last two weeks," Maddie tells me.

"Is it a productive cough?" I ask.

Maddie looks at me blankly.

"Like, does he cough anything up?" I ask.

"Like… phlegm?" She appears horrified at the idea of it.

"Yeah, that's what I was thinking."

"I didn't ask." She glances back at the patient's room. "Should I check?"

"No, please just keep going," I tell her. Maddie's presentations tend to be long and meandering, sometimes involving side trips. I don't want to be here all night.

Correction: I'm definitely going to be here in the hospital all night, since we're on call. But I would rather not be standing in this very spot, listening to Maddie present Mr. Gomez until the sun comes up.

"So the ER doctor thought he had pneumonia," Maddie says. "His lungs sounded… um, junky to me. And her white blood cell count is elevated to 15,000."

"What did the chest X-ray show?" I ask.

That blank look again. "Chest X-ray?"

She's *got* to be messing with me. Even on her second week, an intern should know that you need to look at a chest X-ray to diagnose pneumonia, right? I mean, if you're suspecting an infection of the lungs, you need to look at a picture of the lungs. Even a medical student should know that. Hell, a *child* should know that.

I stare at Maddie, the rant on the tip of my tongue. *How could you not know this by now? How?*

Then I look at the pit stains on her scrubs and I sigh. "Come on," I say, "let's go look at the chest X-ray together."

I just don't have it in me to be mean. Intern year is rough—I don't have to make it worse for her.

Maddie and I discover a large left lower lobe consolidation on Mr. Gomez's chest X-ray and we admit him to County Hospital. My pager goes off just as I'm carefully looking over Maddie's admission orders, making sure she didn't leave off the antibiotics for his pneumonia (like she did last time). I finish double-checking the orders, give her a thumbs-up, then run off to answer my page.

When I dial the number, the person who picks up

the phone doesn't even say hello: "Call room. Ten minutes."

I smile. "I'll be there."

Nine minutes and thirty seconds later, I'm standing in front of the surgery call room. Before I can even knock on the door, it swings open and there he is, looking handsome as ever in his eternal outfit of scrubs. Sexy Surgeon, a.k.a. Dr. Ryan Reilly—my boyfriend. Well, not really my boyfriend. But close enough. Close as I'll ever come when I spend most of my waking hours in the hospital.

He grabs me by the drawstring of my scrubs. "Get in here, you."

I grin up at him. "How long you got?"

"Gotta be in the OR in about twenty minutes. They're going to page me to come down. You?"

"Mm. Maybe half an hour before Maddie screws up and I have to go rescue her."

Ryan laughs. "You need to lay down the line for that girl. Make her *cry*, Jane. It's the only way she'll learn."

That's his answer to everything.

"Is that what you called me here for?" I say. "To give me advice about my intern?"

He leans in to kiss my neck. Well, not my neck, but that sensitive area where my neck meets my shoulder. "No time for that… we've only got twenty minutes…"

We've got twenty minutes in the call room. We've got less than one year until Ryan graduates from his surgical residency here and starts a fellowship in vascular surgery. We've got less than two years until I graduate medicine residency and need to decide what to do with my career. And we've got at least ten years before Ryan starts to show symptoms of the Huntington gene, if he's got it.

But for now, I'm going to enjoy this moment.

Well, at least until my pager goes off.

Hours awake: 18

Chance of quitting: 0.1% (Hey, after spending five freaking years in medical training, what else could I possibly do??)

Chance of living happily ever after:

THE END

ACKNOWLEDGMENTS

First and foremost, I owe a huge thanks to my family for sleeping long enough to allow me time to write this. And also for not spilling anything sticky on my keyboard during the process.

I am eternally grateful to my bestest cyber pals: Dr. Orthochick, Gizabeth, Dr. Grumpy, Carolyn, and Jenica for their advisement, inspiration, and encouragement. I also want to thank Dr. Arnold and Neuro-Trumpet for flashes of inspiration. And a very big thank you to Dr. Katherine Chretien, who introduced me to the wonderful world of blogging. Thank you to Zack, for his tireless help with the Audiobook version of *The Devil Wears Scrubs*.

And finally, I want to thank the real Dr. Alyssa Morgan, for being such a big bitch that I had to write a whole book to complain about you.